Asking Questions Finding Answers

A Parent's Journey through Homeschooling

Asking Questions Finding Answers

A Parent's Journey through Homeschooling

Tamra B. Orr

Asking Questions, Finding Answers:
A Parent's Journey through Homeschooling
by Tamra B. Orr

Published by
　　Home Education Magazine
　　Post Office Box 1083
　　Tonasket, WA 98855
　　(509) 486-1351
　　Orders@homeedmag.com
　　http://www.homeedmag.com

© 2008 HEM Books. All rights reserved. No part of this book may be reproduced or transmitted in any form or by any means, electronic or mechanical, including photocopying, recording or by any information storage and retrieval system without written prior permission from the authors and publishers, except for the inclusion of quotations of not more than 500 words for review purposes only.

First printing 2008.
Printed in the United States of America.

ISBN 978-0-945097-31-0

Library of Congress Cataloging-in-Publication Data

Orr, Tamra
　　Asking Questions, Finding Answers:
　　A Parent's Journey through Homeschooling

　　Includes index.
　　1. Home schooling. 2. Orr, Tamra, 1956-.
　　II. Title.
　　LC40.H44　　　1995　　　　　370.19'3　　88-32018
　　ISBN 978-0-945097-31-0

Acknowledgements

Thanks to the wonderful people who volunteered their time, expertise and passion to write for this book. A big thank you to Mark and Helen for giving me the opportunity to revise, expand and update this book and hopefully, change the world a little by inspiring readers to give homeschooling a try.

Dedication

To the most important people in my world: Jasmine, the first; Nicole, the miracle; Caspian, the son and Coryn, the prize; and to Joseph, my partner in life who made it all possible. Thanks for opening up my eyes to an entirely different world. Walking this pathway together hasn't always been simple, but I couldn't imagine doing it with anyone else.

Foreword

I can't hide my smile when I remember how many school officials, friends, writers, and media commentators considered homeschooling a passing fad in 1981, when I began working with one of the most famous advocates for homeschooling and unschooling, the late John Holt. Most educators and other child experts could not see much growth or promise in a field where one parent had to stay home with the kids with no support from school or government, and all openly-fretted that kids taught this way would have such great gaps in their knowledge that no school, college or work place would accept their homeschooled credentials. Now, 26 years later, homeschooled children are accepted at Ivy League universities, public and private colleges, and the workplace so openly that some families choose homeschooling as a way to add cachet to their childrens' academic records.

Now there are online resources for homeschooling and unschooling, how to courses and seminars offered by local and state homeschooling support groups, books, CDs, videos – even college programs tailored for homeschoolers. Indeed, this wealth of information can be overwhelming for a person seeking knowledge about how to get started with homeschooling. What teaching method should we use? Do I need to buy a curriculum? What groups should we join? Do we need an educational philosophy? What are my state's laws about homeschooling? Can we just wing it? If you have questions like this you can spend hours on the Internet and telephone researching them, or, since you have this book in your hand, you can take a deep breath and settle in for a good read because these, and many questions about homeschooling you may not have formulated yet, are answered thoroughly in this enjoyable collection.

In this book Tamra Orr presents an overview of the development of homeschooling, shares her own experiences as a stay-at-home mom learning with her kids, and presents essays by homeschooling kids, parents, and advocates about their experiences learning together in their homes and communities. These stories are filled with anecdotes, factual information, and lots of resources for discovering your family's style of living and learning together without turning children into stressed-out students and parents into fretful teachers. Read this book as an overview to see the variety of educational experiences that you and your family can have instead of doing conventional schooling at home; use this book as a reference to make homeschooling easier and more enjoyable every day.

Patrick Farenga
President, Holt Associates Inc.
Author, *TEACH YOUR OWN: The John Holt Book of Homeschooling* (Perseus)
January 14, 2008

Patrick Farenga is a consultant and writer about homeschooling, unschooling, and education. He is President of Holt Associates Inc. and the former publisher of Growing Without Schooling magazine. He can be found online at www.holtgws.com, www.learninginourownway.com, and at www.patfarenga.com.

Table of Contents

Foreword— Patrick Farenga

Introduction—The Original (2001)

Introduction—The Sequel (2008)

Chapter 1
How Did Homeschooling Begin and Where is it Going?

How did homeschooling begin?
How many students are being homeschooled?
Why do parents choose to homeschool?
What myths surround homeschooling?
What is homeschooling like for minorities?
What about homeschooling in other countries?
Are there any famous homeschoolers?

In the Trenches
My Evolution in Homeschooling: Martha Lee
Tootsie Roll Decisions: Susan Viator

Voices of Experience
Making the Decision to Homeschool: Mark and Helen Hegener

Chapter 2
Is Homeschooling the Right Choice for our Family?

What qualifications do I need to homeschool?
How much time does homeschooling take?
How much does homeschooling cost?
What about socialization?
What if my child is already in school and I want to start homeschooling?
How can we homeschool if we both work full time?
Can I homeschool some of my children and have others in public school?

Can my child go to homeschool part time and public school part time?
What if my child is doing well in public school?
Want if I am a single parent?
Do moms do all the teaching or do dads have a role in this too?

In the Trenches
On Being a Homeschooling Dad: Gary and Joseph
Socialization: Our Biggest Gripe with Homeschooling: John Anderson
Homeschooling and the Single Parent: Leanne Coffman

Voices of Experience
School through Another Lens: Patrick Farenga

Chapter 3
How Do I Get Started?

Where can I get curricula to use?
Do I teach the same thing/subjects the public schools are teaching?
Can I create my own curricula?
How do I know which grade my child is in?
What does 'deschooling' mean?
What are learning styles?
What is the homeschooling continuum?
Are state tests required? What do I do if they are?
How early or later can I start to homeschool?
Should I go year round or take the summers off?
Do I need to keep records/report cards/documentation on what we do?
How do I homeschool children of different ages and levels?
What role do television and the Internet play in homeschooling?
How can I help my kids stay safe while on the Internet?
How do I teach a subject I dislike or don't understand myself?
How do I know if my child is learning what he/she is 'supposed to'?
How do I keep my children and myself motivated?

In the Trenches
   Homeschooling All Ages: Patti Kurdi
   Homeschooling on Wheels: Peg Wood

Voices of Experience
   Unschooling Adventures: Nancy and Bill Greer

Chapter 4
Where Can I Find Help?

How do I find a local support group?
How do I find a state support group?
How do I find a national support group?
How do I start my own support group?
What kinds of field trips are available?
Why should I go to a homeschool conference?
How do I talk with school officials?
Will the State Department of Education help me?
What if there aren't any homeschoolers close to us?

In the Trenches
   Why a Former School Teacher Chose to Homeschool ~ Francy Stillwell

Voices of Experience
   Dealing with the Rest of the World ~ Pat Montgomery

Chapter 5
How do I Cope with the Rest of the World?

What if my spouse doesn't want to homeschool?
What about unhappy grandparents and other relatives?
What about nosey neighbors and other nuisances?
What happens if my child doesn't want to homeschool?
How do I cope with the questions everyone seems to ask?
How do I deal with hostile or negative school personnel?

In the Trenches
    A Unique Opportunity ~ Carolyn Hoagland

Voices of Experience
    When Methods Collide ~ Teri Brown

Chapter 6
What about the Teen Years?

How do I teach my teen college-prep materials that I don't understand myself?
How does my child get a diploma?
What about graduation?
What about the prom?
How does my homeschooled teen get a job?
What about apprenticeships and internships?
Can my homeschooled teen get into college?
What about playing sports, joining the drama club, being in the orchestra and taking driver's education?

In the Trenches
    The Voices of Youth ~ various teens and young adults

Voices of Experience
    Traveling, Homeschooling and Learning to Relax ~ Jasmine Orr (Part 1)
    Loud Music can Cure Anything ~ Jasmine Pettet (Part 2)

Chapter 7
The What-ifs and What-abouts?

What if my child doesn't have any friends?
What if we have to move?
What if my child wants to go to school?
What if my child never learns to read?
What if my child has to take a test?
What if my child—or I—hate homeschooling?
What if my child is ADD/ADHD?

What if my child is special needs?
What if my child is gifted?

In the Trenches
Some Say ~ Melanie Walenciak
Homeschooling Your Special Needs Child ~ Deborah Bradshaw

Voices of Experience
World Championship Homeschooling ~ Bill Ward

Chapter 8
What are the Legalities?

How do the laws differ from state to state?
How do I know what the laws are in my state?

In the Trenches
Our Self-Education Adventure ~ Letha McGee
Long Pregnancy, Big Baby ~ Nicholina O'Donnell

Voices of Experience
Is Homeschooling Legal? ~ Larry and Susan Kaseman

About the Author

Introduction—The Original (2001)

My personal journey to homeschooling is much like that taken by many homeschoolers. I started out with the simple step of becoming a mother and discovering quickly that everything I thought about children and how they should be raised was basically wrong. As in the words of John Wilmot, Earl of Rochester, "Before I got married I had six theories about bringing up children; now I have six children and no theories." My first child—now ironically referred to as my walking homeschooling audio-visual material—opened my eyes to many aspects of being a parent that I had never given thought to before. The pathway my husband and I found ourselves following was not the typical, traditional one that we saw mirrored in our society's culture; instead, it was one that was based on what our hearts and our daughter's spirit told us. It wasn't always popular with friends and relatives, but we still knew it was the right direction to go, and we leaned on each other when others tried to persuade us to detour.

One of the integral steps along that parenting pathway was discovering homeschooling. In 1988, it was still on the fringe and far from being the accepted model of education it is now becoming but that was part of its appeal. When we first heard of it, we were intrigued. Both of us had had negative school experiences and we did not want this for our children. I had a brand new teaching degree under my arm and knew that I could teach my daughter better than anyone else could—after all, I had already helped her with the hard stuff—she knew how to walk, talk, feed herself and get dressed. We hadn't needed a teacher for that, so why did we need one now? The thought of having this six year old child gone from me all day was so bizarre and unnatural; I couldn't imagine how other parents did it. So, my husband and I made the choice to homeschool.

That was 18 years ago. Our walking AV material has been traveling the country for three years now, being remarkably independent and, as she puts it, "Out seeing the world instead of just reading about it." Since then, three more children have come along to open our eyes about more things and to teach us more lessons than I can count. Through it all, our belief in homeschooling and what it does for a person, a family, and the world has only deepened. It is my joy that I can write this book and hopefully, through what you read and learn here, you might make the same choice for your family also. I can think of no better way to share the power of home education.

A note to remember as you read all of the "In the Trenches" essays—they represent a huge scope of homeschooling ideas, methods, feelings and thoughts. Some will strike you as right; some as wrong. What these essays are meant to show is that there is *no one right way* to homeschool; there are as many different philosophies and approaches as there are families. While one essay may advocate one direction, another might come along that supports the opposite path. I personally might have been cheering as I read one and shaking my head as I read another. These essays are simply intended to bring you into the minds of homeschoolers across the country and show you their incredible diversity.

Also, here and there throughout the book, I refer to homeschooling as a movement. For some, this word implies change; it infers options or choices. For others, it means fanaticism or radicalism. As used in this book, the homeschooling movement refers to the entire population of homeschoolers, whether they identify themselves politically or not, as well as the laws and the culture that have grown up around homeschooling.

Homeschooling is a journey for all those who choose to take it. This book is a reflection of what I have learned on that journey, and I hope that it can act as a road map that makes your trip easier. There are no mandatory routes; detours are almost inevitable and can be the best part. Plot your course, grab your compass, and start the expedition. Wishing you many delightful discoveries!

Introduction—The Sequel (2008)

I wrote that introduction six—almost seven—years ago. As I read it over again while preparing this all new edition of the former A Parent's Guide to Homeschooling, it still rings very true to me. This homeschooling life choice has been quite the journey.

Today, my walking AV material (Jasmine) is married (to another unschooler) and working in the social services arena. Low pay, long hours, heartbreaking stories and a drive to help the world become a better place. She contributes a good share of gray hairs for me with her stories of working with meth addicts, rape victims and other lost souls.

My next daughter (Nicole) is just 17 and is involved in so many activities that my date book somehow turned into her social calendar. Along with the typical teen activities like meeting friends and hanging out in coffee shops, she has been involved in martial arts classes, dragon boating, ballroom dance, Girl Scouts, a myriad of summer camps (including the infamous Not Back to School Camp where she, like her older sister, found a second home), Habitat for Humanity, National Novel Writing Month (a/k/a NaNoWriMo) and even a few jobs here and there. Her future is leaning towards a career in some kind of urban search and rescue work. She just joined the county division and I marvel that my triple-chinned, pudgy-thighed baby is now this long, lean thing out braving the wild with a grin on her face.

My boys are 14 (Caspian) and 11 (Coryn) now. The older one learned to read at 13 and hasn't stopped since; his younger brother learned at 7 and reads faster than lightning. They play World of Warcraft and other video games together and are each other's best friend. Caspian's voice dropped an octave and he grew a foot overnight I swear. I can just see a flicker of the little boy in there, covered up by the immense shadow of the man he is becoming. Coryn is the family intellectual, whipping out vocabulary words that startle all of us and throwing about phrases like, "I'm a force not to be trifled with" with great panache.

Homeschooling is such a part of us now that we cannot imagine life any other way. Ironically, in both places we have lived (Indiana and now Oregon), we have been only a matter of blocks from several public schools. We hear the practice sessions of their bands, the whistles of football coaches and the yelling and laughter of kids at recess from our back yards. We are inundated with the sounds of school buses picking up in the morning and dropping off in the afternoon. Daily, students walk by the house talking, laughing, yelling, fighting, singing and thinking. They seem to be in a different world than we are sometimes. We all like our world a lot better.

Since moving to Oregon (just as the first edition of this book went to press), our lives have certainly changed for the better. Out here we are surrounded by a wonderful homeschooling community that loves and accepts us without asking if we go to church first. We have secular friends, religious friends and somewhere-in-between friends. We have so many opportunities for our children to take classes, attend workshops, meet people and socialize, that we feel very grateful.

In the almost seven years since I wrote the first edition of this book, I have traveled the country several times and talked to many, many homeschoolers or wanna-be homeschoolers. I went on two national book tours and spoke at bookstores, on television and on radio. (For a person who used to be too shy to order a pizza over the phone, this was *quite* an achievement!) I met hostile fathers, worried mothers, timid kids, outspoken teenagers, both misguided and sincere reporters and wonderful families on these trips. I saw everything from scuba diving classes in an L.A. hotel pool to a baptism in an Oklahoma hotel pool. I went on shows where the host asked an honest question and then sat back to listen thoughtfully to my answer and others where before I could reply, the host was already taking over, rendering me superfluous. When I was finally done with all the traveling, I came back to Portland and over the last few years, have been in local newspapers and TV shows whenever I am involved in workshops—or publishing a book. Throughout all of this, I have been struck by several things:

• Parents, regardless of their beliefs, attitudes and backgrounds really all want one thing: the best for their children.
• Homeschooling has come a long way—it doesn't raise eyebrows at all like it used to when I started back in the 1980s.
• The world is an amazing place to learn if we just get out of the way and allow it to happen.

When revising and updating this edition, I toyed with changing the format away from questions and answers but, in the end, decided to leave it as is. I originally chose this format because when I was searching for information, I had specific questions I wanted answered and I got frustrated with books that I had to wade through to get to that answer. I hope to help readers avoid that by putting this in the Q and A format. Flip right to the question you want to read and then go from there.

As I said seven years ago, enjoy the journey!

Chapter 1

How Did Homeschooling Begin —and Where is it Going?

"How we learn is what we learn."
~ Bonnie Friedman, essay writer

Consider this chapter your basic 101 course in homeschooling. It will give you a good grounding in where homeschooling came from, who helped it along and who has taken its tenets and made it a part of their lives.

How did Homeschooling Begin?

Homeschooling is not a new concept but just a revival of the main form of education that took place in this country before the mid-19th century—up until then, most children stayed at home and learned all of the essentials of life, from how to make soap and milk cows to how to read and write well enough to communicate. In 1852, the state of Massachusetts set the first state compulsory school attendance law and other states followed after that, much to outrage of many families. To the surprise of many people, the words "school" and "education" are nowhere to be found in the Declaration of Independence, the Constitution or the Bill of Rights.

As the world shifted to a more industrial society, mass-producing competent workers became a higher priority and for this, school was deemed necessary. It stayed that way until the early 1960s when a few dissenting voices were heard. Inspired by the writings of Ivan Illich's *Deschooling Society* and Harold Bennet's *No More Public School,* a former teacher and homeschool forefather John Holt wrote *How Children Fail,* a serious look at how schools were damaging children. His other books, such as *Instead of Education: Ways to Help People Do Things Better* and *Teach Your Own: A Hopeful Path for Education,* along with his magazine, *Growing without Schooling*, helped support families who wanted to give their children strong educations that did not involve conventional schooling. It was followed in 1983 by the publication *Home Education Magazine*, another homeschooling magazine that focused on encouraging homeschoolers. A few years later, Dr. Raymond Moore, a former employee of the U.S. Department of Education, and his wife Dorothy, a teacher, began talking to over a hundred child development specialists about how schooling was affecting young children. Their groundbreaking research led to numerous books such as *Better Late than Early, School can Wait* and *Home Grown Kids* and their strong advocacy of homeschooling which continues into today, despite the loss of Dr. Moore. They strongly supported the idea of delaying formal education for a child until at least ten years old.

A landmark court case occurred in 1978 *(Perchemlides v. Frizzle)* when a Massachusetts court upheld the right of a family to homeschool their son. The 1980s brought even more momentum to the homeschooling movement. Changes in tax regulations forced many small, private, Christian schools to close, and a number of these families chose the homeschooling option over sending their children to public school.

In 1983 David and Micki Colfax became celebrities when their homeschooled son Grant was accepted into Harvard—this put homeschooling into the media more than ever before as the family appeared on television talk shows and in magazine and newspaper articles; in subsequent years younger sons Drew and Reed, also homeschooled, went off to Harvard as well.

By 1986, all 50 states allowed homeschooling, as they do today. As each decade passes, the interest in homeschooling increases. Studies are being done, books are being written, interviews are being conducted and slowly, but surely, the concept of teaching your children at home has become an acceptable one for many. In 2001, it even made the cover of *Time* magazine, asking the question "Is Homeschooling Good for America?" Home education continues to be a topic that the media explores on a regular basis. As people read about the incidents of violence taking place in schools today, they are also beginning to wonder if homeschooling is not only a better option for their children, but also a safer one.

How Many Students are Being Homeschooled?

The answer to this one boils down to this: it depends on whom you ask. I remember speaking on the phone with the head of my (then) state's department of education, asking how many homeschoolers she thought there were in our state. She said she had about 200 registered, so that must be accurate. With a wicked grin, I asked her if she knew that the last state homeschooling conference had more than 2,000 people attending. She didn't. She was also temporarily speechless.

The fact of the matter is that homeschooling statistics are out there; unfortunately, that does not mean the truth is out there as well. The statistics surrounding homeschooling are always changing and rarely accurate. Each organization that estimates the number bases that estimate on different criteria and many of the numbers simply are not reliable. One group, for example, may base their numbers on how many families are registered with state departments of education, while others might base it on a survey they created and sent out. Others may base estimates on sales of curricula or other homeschooling related products and services. The problem with this is that there are quite a few homeschoolers who do not register, take surveys or buy a curriculum. These are homeschoolers who prefer to keep a low profile. They don't want others interfering in what they are doing, and they suspect that much of the research being done will only end up doing harm to homeschoolers instead of helping them.

These families are not necessarily being paranoid either. There is a strong feeling among some that research on homeschooling might be detrimental both to the concept of homeschooling and to individual families. According to Larry and Susan Kaseman, authors and columnists for *Home Education Magazine*, almost all survey questions are based on the public school model of education. Researchers are looking for grades, hours spent teaching specific subjects, types of curriculum, and other attributes of public school. All these concepts are public school concepts and may not play a part in a family's homeschooling style at all. This can make homeschooling parents begin to doubt themselves as they are led to look to the public school system as the one to emulate in their homes—an idea that is rarely, if ever, true. Instead of looking at what homeschoolers do well in their own style, these surveys look only at how they are doing in comparison to their public schooled peers. "Research is doing homeschooling more harm than good," the Kasemans write. "Homeschoolers seldom benefit from it. Instead, the benefits go to researchers, universities, attorneys and others who use it in place of direct knowledge, alternative practices and effective political action."

What all of this means, of course, is that, at this time, there is no study that can definitely state how many homeschoolers there are in this country. There are simply too many homeschooling families out there who are being overlooked as they homeschool under the radar.

Why Do Parents Choose to Homeschool?

In some ways, there is no way to answer this question. It is a little like asking why parents choose to have a child. Every single person you ask will have a slightly different answer. The ones listed here are the most general ones—most likely, it is a combination of several with different angles and attitudes mixed in. These are the reasons I have personally encountered while interviewing families, meeting hundreds of them on tours, reading and researching, talking to personal friends, and exploring my own pathway.

For example, the reasons my husband and I chose to homeschool were primarily because we had had some pretty miserable public school experiences. I had been perpetually bullied. I had trouble reading (a fact that still gives me an ironic giggle today). I didn't have any friends. I dreaded school with a passion for the first seven years. In junior high and high school, things were better. I found a niche and stayed there (smart enough to be in honors but not to be a geek; enough friends to have fun but far too few and not the right ones to be popular.) When I thought of our first child possibly having to face some of the same treatment I had, I couldn't do it. It was like throwing her to the wolves and hoping she had enough sense to run fast.

As for my husband, his school experiences were less than enjoyable also. Like me, he was bullied. He found himself hanging with the ones no one else wanted to hang with and wondering why. He was bored and could never understand why he was even in school—what was the point? He still says he just didn't have a clue as to what was happening around him socially (again amazing, as this is the *most* social man I have ever met in my life now!).

Here are the main reasons I have heard people state:

- *Dissatisfaction with the public school system.* Whether they are upset with the curriculum, the teachers, the standards, or everything in between, parents almost always cite unhappiness with the school as one of their main reasons for looking at other options.

- *A noticeable decline in a child's spirit/enthusiasm/love of learning.* One of the warning signs that something is amiss with a child's education is when a child suddenly stops wanting to learn Parents may see their children spending more time in front of the television than reading books, declining grades, increasing frustration with homework or other telltale signs. A child may act more restless, unhappy or bored at home and may develop a need to be entertained, rather than entertaining himself. All of these can be signs there is a problem. A child is born with a drive to learn and if that drive is fading, something is wrong.

This point was driven home to me by one of my friends. She has been a Girl Scout leader for many years—as well as a homeschooler. In the beginning, her troop was made up of almost all public schooled students, other than her own daughter. "The first year of Daisies, my girls would come in and I would have a table set up with glitter, stickers, paper, scissors and other craft materials," she said. "They would have the best time talking, creating and imagining and go home with their masterpiece. The following year, after they had been in first grade, they came in and sat at the table and made something, but with less enthusiasm. The following year, they came in and began making something, but kept comparing it to the others to see if it was 'as good'. By the fourth year, they came in, sat down at the table and waited to be told what to do with the material."

- *A child in some type of trouble.* This so-called trouble could be anything from low grades to high absenteeism, or it can be a problem with behavior in the classroom. Some parents find themselves looking at homeschooling after their children have been suspended or expelled. Others see falling grades of skipping school as a problem that might be handled better at home.
- *A child is not fitting in.* Many children are shaped in ways that just do not fit the typical public school mold. They might have a learning disability; they might be gifted—or both. They majority of schools simply are not set up to address these situations as well as a loving family can. Many families prefer to educate their gifted, disabled, or special children at home, rather than to entrust them to a system that is designed to meet the needs of the average child.
- *Religious/spiritual reasons.* A significant portion of the families who homeschool today do so for religious reasons. They want the basic tenets of their faith—whatever faith it might be—to be an integral part of their children's curriculum and overall life perspectives. By home educating, they can select lessons and other materials that support their religious stance, and they can build in ethics and morals without fear of exposing their children to concepts they do not believe. Now that I am updating this book, I added the word "spiritual" to this reason. I did this because I have recently met a number of families who are not the traditional religious people. Instead, these families follow pathways of pagan, Islamic, Buddhist and other spiritual choices that do not fall into the typical formats. But, just like other families, they homeschool, at least partially, in orderto support these beliefs and traditions.

- *To keep a child safe.* Sadly, one of the reasons that homeschooling has seen a rise in interest in recent years is due to the horrible incidents of school violence. Newspapers run stories after each event remarking on the surge of interest in home education. Parents may indeed fear their children are at risk after incidents like Columbine and Virginia Tech, but there are a number of risks more common than a tragic figure with a gun. Families may worry about their children being at risk from other things, including pressure from peers to take drugs, drink alcohol or have sex. While homeschooling certainly doesn't guarantee these things won't happen, it will definitely limit the opportunities and the temptations for them to happen.

A side detour from the author again—I was hired by Scholastic to write a book about school violence. I did (*School Violence: Halls of Hope, Halls of Fear*) and it actually won a pretty prestigious award from New York City Community Public Library who named it the best nonfiction book for teens for 2004. Anyway—I put a couple of paragraphs about homeschooling in it as one of the options families can consider if worried about their children's safety. I got some flack from the editors, but I stood by what I said, and it was included in the book. I still feel good about that one.

- *Build family bonds.* Some families choose homeschooling simply because they don't like having the family separated for eight-plus hours per day. Siblings rarely see each other, and mom and dad are often too busy working, making meals and doing household chores and errands to spend much one-on-one time with their children. Homeschooling means more time together to work not only on something educational, but to talk, wonder, dream, discuss and share. Many times the outcome is a closer family that understands and likes each other. They all share common daily experiences, rather than spending the day separate from each other in different activities. Frequently, by being together everyday, siblings have stronger relationships.

- *Overall superior education.* Lastly, many parents truly believe that they can give their children a better education than the school can. They have the time and the interest, as well as an in-depth knowledge of their children's strengths, weaknesses and learning styles. They can design an educational program that fits the child rather than forcing the child to fit the educational style. Homeschooling is flexible, affordable and has a terrific student-to-teacher ratio!

What Myths Surround Homeschooling?

A number of common myths or misconceptions surround the concept of homeschooling. Many of them, just like the stories found screaming across the tabloids, may have started out with a nugget of truth and then, somewhere down the line, become skewed and false. Here are a few of the most typical myths that still haunt the movement:

• *Only hippies homeschool.* When people originally heard about homeschooling several decades ago, they usually attributed the movement to parents who refused to leave behind the 'question authority' attitude of the 1960s and 1970s or to families who lived in such remote areas of the world that they had no choice in the matter. While those families may have been some of the forerunners of home education, it is certainly no longer true today. Families of all kinds homeschool now—married and single, religious and secular, rich and poor, black, white, yellow or red. They are from all ethnic and social backgrounds with any range of political leanings. They share one main aspect: they are parents looking for a better educational option than public school for their children.

• *Only Christians homeschool.* This is a common thought in recent years because many of the homeschooling families who are profiled in the media are from the Christian faith. However, perpetuating the myth means that people of other faiths and who those who are agnostic/atheist are being ignored. While quite a few of the homeschoolers today do tend to follow one of a number of faiths, from Christian to Mormon to Islamic, the number of secular homeschoolers is growing steadily and should not be overlooked.

• *Homeschooling is school brought home.* It certainly can be organized just like a classroom—from recess periods to report cards, bells to pop quizzes. However, it can also be intentionally designed to be absolutely nothing like traditional school. Just like there is no one absolute way to parent, there is no one absolute way to homeschool. The hours, style, curriculum and all other details depend entirely on the needs, interests and personalities of the most important people in the picture—the parents and their children. One of the biggest advantages to homeschooling is that the whole design of it is in your hands and under your control. You set the pace, the direction, the schedule and style in the way that best fits your children and you. For some families, this may mean something modeled directly like public school; for others (like me!), it is directly the opposite or somewhere in between.

• *You have to have a teaching degree to homeschool.* Take my personal word for it—if you do, it's harder, not better. And it is not a legal requirement either. I have a teaching degree, and it was the first thing I had to unlearn when I left the classroom and started working with my first child. I will always remember the impact of sitting in my first homeschooling conference (thanks, Clonlara!) and the question was asked at the key note address of how many people in the audience were current or former teachers. Wow, where there a lot of hands. Shows you the confidence we all had in the school system, doesn't it? Those with teaching degrees, like me, found that while college taught them how to teach, their own children were teaching them how to learn.

• *Homeschooling is expensive.* Sure, it can be—but it doesn't have to be! Part of what will determine the cost of homeschooling in your family is the style you use. The more formal you are or the more you chose to imitate public school, the more materials you will need and thus the more it may cost. Those families who are more relaxed or who lean more to unschooling, on the other hand, will have far less expenses. You can buy materials from curriculum companies, but be sure to check out cheaper alternatives like thrift stores, garage sales and teacher supply stores.

• *Homeschooling isn't legal.* As of 1986, it has been legal to homeschool in every state of the U.S. The laws and regulations are governed by the individual states, however, so there are different restrictions and requirements you need to know about.

• *Homeschooled children won't learn how to socialize.* If you want to see a homeschooler grit his/her teeth, just ask the question, "What about socialization?" Trust me—this is the least of your worries. A homeschooling father I met once said, "Yes! Socializing IS a problem. There is so much of it, I have to figure out what to say no to!" Another mom says, tongue in check, "Sure, I make sure my kids get public school socialization. Every other day I beat them up and steal their lunch money!" The real world, where people of varying ages, sizes, backgrounds and styles live, is not in a classroom. Homeschooled children learn about the world by being involved in it, rather than studying about in a textbook.

What is Homeschooling Like for Minority Families?

According to the U.S. Department of Education, minorities (Asians, Hispanics, African-Americans, Native Americans and Jews) make up one quarter of the total homeschooling population. The problems these groups face are sometimes slightly different. A minority within a minority, they often deal with feelings of isolation and lack of support. For instance, some African-Americans have been condemned for homeschooling when their heritage includes such a strong fight to get into public schools. For some, homeschooling seems like a betrayal. Joyce and Eric Burges, who founded the National Black Home Educators in 2000 in Baker, Louisiana, say their mission is to "empower parents to educate their children for excellence" (www.nbhe.net).

Other support groups include the African American Homeschoolers Network (www.aahnet.org) , the African American Unschooling site (www.afamunschool.com) and the Black Homeschoolers' Network (blackhomeschoolers.homestead.com). For more resources, check out http://homeschooling.gomilpitas.com/religion/afrocentric.htm.

What about homeschooling in other countries?

Homeschooling is taking hold in other countries, as well as in the U.S. It has reached Australia, France, the U.K, South Africa, Israel and Japan and continues to spread further each year. To find out more, check *Home Education Magazine's* resource list found at http://homeedmag.com/groups/orgs.html#International.
Additional resources can be found at http://homeschooling.gomilpitas.com/regional/Europe.htm.

Are there any Famous Homeschoolers?

As Grace Llewellyn wrote in her book, *The Teenage Liberation Handbook,* "One third of the men who signed the Declaration of Independence, the Articles of Confederation and the Constitution of the United States, had no more than a few months of schooling up their sleeves." Many of this country's presidents, senators and other government officials were homeschooled, as were a number of military leaders and Supreme Court judges. In addition to them, here are a few other recognizable names.

- Albert Einstein, scientist
- Booker T. Washington, scientist
- Leonardo da Vinci, artist
- Thomas Edison, inventor
- Orville and Wilbur Wright, inventors
- Hans Christian Anderson, author
- Samuel Clemens/Mark Twain, author
- Alex Haley, author
- L. Ron Hubbard, author
- Christopher Paolini, author
- Charlie Chaplin, actor
- Whoopi Goldberg, actress/comedian
- Jennifer Love Hewitt, actress
- LeAnne Rimes, singer
- Venus and Sarina Williams, athletes
- Dakota Fanning, actress
- Jena Malone, actress
- JoJo, singer and actress

In the Trenches

My Evolution in Homeschooling ~ Martha Lee

How I think about public schools has changed dramatically over the years since I began homeschooling my eldest son nine years ago, following an unpleasant kindergarten experience. I went from being afraid to do something so radical, to wondering how anyone can put up with the subtle disrespect schools give parents and children alike. I went from believing that schools are necessary, to knowing they are ludicrous. In recent years, I have been known to say things like, "My children have committed no crime, so I decided not to incarcerate them!" When I drive past a public school now, they seem as foreign as prisons to me. After all, both are large institutions where people are kept in an orderly and often dehumanizing manner against their wills. I try not to fully admit my radical views to my three children, in the event our lifestyle changes one day and they are forced to go to school. Instead, I just focus on giving them their freedom and dignity to learn in a relaxed atmosphere of caring.

There are many things that schools provide that people think of as necessary, but are they really? Most parents worry about the socialization issue, for example. Will homeschoolers learn to get along with their peers? After nine years of homeschooling, I believe that too much of the socialization kids receive in school is actually quite detrimental. My kids have plenty of contact with peers through 4-H, scouting, church, neighborhood kids, family, friends, and relatives. I live in Lansing, Michigan, and we have a large homeschool support group that meets at the main library downtown. My friend and I founded the group three years ago, and now we have 80 families on our mailing list. Homeschoolers come from all over the greater Lansing area every week to this center of learning for socialization, board games, arts and crafts, and other activities where outside teachers teach subjects that are beyond the realm of parents.

I once thought, will I know enough to be able to teach my own kids all the way through the challenging years of high school? I have seen other mothers do it, and I realize it is because they were learning right along with their children. Homeschooling parents are one intelligent and educated group of people!

I asked myself, What about tests? Can my children survive without them? A homeschooling friend of mine once ran into a truancy officer in the city. He asked her about testing and she replied, "Tests are for schools where there are 30 kids in a class, and the kids change teachers every year. It is the only way to keep track of where all those individual children are in their progress. I don't need them because I know exactly where each of my children is in their learning." The truancy officer never questioned her again.

I wondered about textbooks; did I need to go to the expense of providing the same ones the school did? I thought for years that textbooks were a necessary evil, but I don't think that anymore. In my family, we go to public libraries and borrow books on the same topics covered in science, history, and social studies and somehow, these books are so much more interesting. Textbooks almost seem designed to kill the interest of any curious mind. I found that most math textbooks, for example, have a great deal of unneeded repetition and busy work in them. I think they are created this way to keep children occupied in the classroom, more as a matter of crowd control than learning. My children and I prefer the math books that cover a topic fully from the beginning to end, one that completely covers the concept of addition, subtraction, fractions, etc. We like to use many of the creative alternatives to textbooks in our homeschooling, and that's one of the nicest things about learning at home—there are so many choices.

One advantage to homeschooling that I hadn't anticipated when I first started was that homeschooled children do not seem to suffer the same burnout that their public school peers often do. They have more time to spend on outside interests, like music or martial arts. My son's Tae Kwon Do teacher told me that his homeschooled students seemed more studious. Institutionally schooled kids have to deal with following rules all day—from sitting and paying attention to the teacher, to asking permission to go to the bathroom. They are surrounded with regimentation and coercion to follow the rules the entire time they are in school. My sons can go to their lessons with a fresher attitude, with noticeable results.

Learning styles can vary greatly from one child to the next, even in the same family. Schools basically use one primary method, but that doesn't work for all children. Some learn better while music is playing or while they are moving around. In our homeschooling environment, education is individualized to meet each child's needs and styles.

Discipline was a huge concern for my parents when we announced our plans to homeschool. It is sometimes easy for me to lose sight of regimentation and structure in homeschooling. Now, after years of observing my children and how they learn and work, I see that when they are interested in something, they dive into it with passion. Discipline becomes irrelevant. I make sure I have learning materials readily available, and when the urge strikes them, they pick the things up and begin to study on their own, with interest. What I am seeing is that when I do not impose outside structure, my children develop their own self-discipline, based on enthusiasm and not coercion. Children naturally enjoy doing things well when they are not being forced to do so. When they are led by their own sense of wonder, they learn easily and with happiness. Having grown up in a household where discipline was highly valued, it was a true lesson for me to recognize that it is okay to be flexible. My children can work for long hours on a project that fascinates them, or they can begin their writing lessons at 8 p.m. rather than 9 a.m. Why not? There is no need to schedule learning because my kids are doing it all the time.

   I will never forget my son's compelling question his first week of kindergarten. He asked, "Do they love me at school?" I hemmed and hawed, trying to find the right answer to this difficult question, but he kept pressing me. "Yes, I know they like me and they want the best for me," he continued, "but do they *love* me?" He had never been to preschool and had only been left in the care of grandparents or aunts for babysitters, so he was struggling to understand why he suddenly had to go and spend so much time with people he didn't know. After all of these years, I realize that there is no good reason to put children with strangers when they can do their schoolwork and learning at home in the company of those that love them most. What better way to foster self-esteem? My son's tender question put it all in perspective for me.

   I often mention to my kids that homeschooling is not all it can be in the world, that as it evolves, it will improve. Communities will support it more one day, and it will become more widely accepted. As this happens, our very notions of education will evolve and improve, for the benefit of children everywhere. Homeschooling shook up my belief system, and I understand from an all-new perspective why government officials worry about education reform. Homeschoolers may well have a lot of answers to that problem, and one day, I believe, the "experts" will even ask for our advice.

In the Trenches

Tootsie Roll Decisions ~ Susan Viator

   When Matt started kindergarten, he already knew his letters, his numbers, name, address, shapes and colors. (This was before the day when kindergartners were tested to make sure they know calculus and could read *War and Peace* if they wanted to be promoted to first grade.) Since he was bored with lessons, his teacher immediately played the attention deficit card.

   "I'm a little concerned about Matthew. He seems to have trouble sitting still for lessons and sometimes behaves inappropriately. I think it's possible he *is* ADD."

   I think it's possible he *is* a child, I thought.

   She suggested I have him evaluated by the district for a possible learning problem. (A five year old is having trouble sitting still and sometimes acts, well, five? What should we DO?!)

In the same smarmy tone of voice the teacher had used, fake concern apparent on my face, I said, "Let me set your mind at ease. I wouldn't want you to worry over Matt. That's not his problem. He's bored. He already knows what you're teaching."

Soon after school started, he came home talking about his new friend, Miss Brittleface, the school counselor. Miss Brittleface had invited the children, three at a time, to her office. She told the children that she was their friend, and that if they ever had problems, even at home, she would be there to talk to. She explained that she knew how hard it could be to talk to Mommy or Daddy sometimes because they don't always understand. This was all reported to me by my five year old. He said he knew he could talk to HIS mom and dad, but that some kids didn't have any other friends, so it was nice that she was there. I hated having him in school, and had already begun to think about homeschooling, but I knew it was something my husband Eric would never agree to.

My daughter Lyssa was born that summer. Matt didn't want to go to school and leave us. He couldn't understand why, since he'd learned to read that summer, he had to go to school.

I said all of the things that parents say.

"You need to go to school so you can learn."

"Big boys your age go to school! That's what they all do!"

"We'll still be here when you come home from school. We'll miss you, too!"

At open house, I spoke with Matt's teacher while Eric toured the classroom. I asked her how things were going for Matt. With a tight-lipped, tense smile on her face, she said, "Well, I don't know about Matthew. He has a real problem sitting still. AND! He's been reversing a few letters! I wonder if we don't have a little attention deficit on our hands. He thinks it's funny to play with the light switches! He talks in the hall! He chases girls on the playground!"

Imagine how horrified I was to hear that he was behaving like a normal child! Wow, had I done a horrible job as a parent or what? Somehow, I hid my anguish. "You know, I think he may be bored," I suggested.

I know I don't have total recall. But these words are burned forever into my brain. She answered, "No, he isn't bored. Not if he's as smart as I think he is. No truly intelligent person is EVER bored." I disagree. When you're a captive six-year-old, boredom is probably pretty high on the list of things affecting you.

After talking with my son after school every day, seeing the very rudimentary work he brought home, and seeing the attitude of his teacher toward him, I became very sure he didn't belong in her class. I went to visit the principal. I explained my dissatisfaction with the simplistic work Matt had been doing, mentioned his normal childhood behaviors of trying to make other kids laugh and chasing girls, and pointed out that in the 10 minutes I had talked with his teacher, she hadn't said one single positive thing about my son. Of course, he did what he's paid to do; he supported the teacher. He said that before he'd consider moving my child to another class, perhaps I'd agree to meet with her?

I grew up in a home with a teacher father and a school bus driver mom. Only a fool would show no willingness to work with the staff! (Now, it horrifies me when I think of how accommodating I was willing to be.) We scheduled a meeting. I carefully assembled the work and projects he had done at home. I stayed up late the night before, worrying over what I would say and making notes so I wouldn't forget the points I wanted to make. I went in with my best friendly look on my face, and acted like the best parent I could. I was so nice to them that, after a little persuasion, I agreed to leave my child in that class! Please don't think less of me. I loved my little boy and wanted the best for him. I just didn't know how to play the game as well as I thought I did.

From that point on, the teacher kept her eye on Matt. I had questioned her teaching skills and she wasn't about to let me forget. Worse, she was taking it out on him in subtle little ways. Every day, she walked out with him after school and listed all the things he had done wrong.

"Matt made inappropriate noises in the hallway."

"Matt spoke out of turn in class!"

"Matt was play fighting on the playground!"

All of those things were normal kid behaviors, and I was *embarrassed* about them! We disciplined him for it.

Matt, you can't act up at school. Didn't we teach you better manners?"

"No Legos for a week."

We were making ourselves sick over the situation. We would lie awake at night, discussing ways to make him behave at school. It was ugly. We got up in the morning and served him a dose of "Straighten up your act" along with his breakfast. He went to school and was squelched all day long. I was waiting to pounce the moment he walked out the door of the school, and the moment his dad came home from work, we rehashed the entire day.

Then, during one of our night conversations, we began discussing home- schooling. At first it was my idea. I figured since I was home with the baby anyway, it would be simple. Eric was totally and completely against the idea. "He'll be socially retarded!"

Our agonizing had one positive result, though. We relaxed our attitude about Matt's behavior. He began to feel better, and it showed.

In April, we decided that maybe homeschooling would be a good thing. We didn't feel like the public school was helping him reach his potential. The only advanced work we'd seen all year was a report on the planets he'd done at home with his dad. It seemed reasonable that we could offer him more than the school could.

The final factor in our decision was this.

His teacher asked me to help my son's class with a papier mache project. As I stood in the back of the room, up to my elbows in glue, tissue paper and kids, I got to witness the excitement as Miss Brittleface skipped into the room holding a big clear bag of Tootsie Rolls. Wow. That was some bag. She almost needed a wagon.

"Where are all my good boys and girls?" she called out joyously. "I have something special for you!"

She then handed out candy to eight children, told them how wonderful they were, and waltzed out of the room after ignoring the rest. The special children opened the candy, stuffed it into their mouths, and ate it in front of the rest of the class. It's not even possible to describe the disappointment on the faces of the other kids.

Stunned, but still in good-parent mode, I said nothing until we arrived home from school that afternoon and I was able to question my son. He explained that in the morning, his teacher had been out of the classroom for a while. Miss Brittleface sat in for her, and told the class that if they sat quietly and colored their pictures, she would give them "something wonderful!"

"I was really good, too!" he said. "And she didn't even notice me!"

Well, I was so angry I didn't trust myself to call the school. I waited a whole night, called my friends, ranted to my hubby, and stewed over it instead of sleeping for a good portion of the night. Food as a reward? Group rewards? Group punishments for the others? I was ready to tackle the issue the next morning, and called Miss Brittleface. She agreed to see me right away.

She was pleased to see me. I know this because she offered me the big, professional smile, touched me on the arm and invited me into her little office. She even gave me the nice chair!

"What can I do for you today?" she asked.

"Well, you could explain for me the Tootsie Roll theory of discipline," I replied.

She offered a puzzled little smile. "I'm not sure what you mean."

"Well, I saw the little one act play in my son's class yesterday, and I was just a little curious about it."

"Oh!" she exclaimed. Enunciating most carefully, and leaning closer so she could help me understand, she continued. "That's called *positive reinforcement*." She gave me a conspiratorial pat on the arm.

"No, it's not called positive reinforcement." I said. "It's called operant conditioning, and is an excellent tool for training a dog. I fail to see how you can regard anything as positive when it causes so many negative feelings. Do you even have any children?"

"Why yes I do!" she exclaimed, quickly donning what I assume was supposed to be a proud, maternal smile. Since this was the same smile she had used while tossing Tootsie Rolls, when welcoming me to her office and to denote puzzlement, I was not convinced it was genuine.

"I have a daughter in the second grade!"

"How nice. Does she go to school here?"

"Why no!" she exclaimed. "My daughter is in a private school!"

"How nice. How would you feel if she came home from school feeling as bad as my son did yesterday?"

"Well," she confided with another pat on my arm. "My daughter is quite talkative. I can easily see how we could have a situation like that. I might then ask her what she could do to get a Tootsie Roll the next time."

"Well, all my son has to do is tell me," I smiled. "And I'll go buy him a whole bag!"

"OH!" she exclaimed. "Don't you think that undermines what we're trying to do here? We must have some checks and balances, we have a lot of children here, and they must conform!"

"Okay," I said. "What if I go buy a bag of Hershey's kisses and tell my son to bring them to school and hand them out only to the kids he likes. Is that okay?"

"Oh no! That would be unfair!"

"Well, don't you think what you're doing is unfair? I haven't taught my son to behave that way. The way I see it, you're undermining ME."

We took Matt out of school after first grade. He never went back. He's in college now and doing well. He no longer plays with light switches in the classroom, speaks out of turn, or chases girls on the playground. He has a job dealing with the public, so it seems he is able to communicate. He has a girlfriend. He has many friends to hang out with. Hardly socially retarded.

The Voice Of Experience

"I have never let my schooling interfere with my education."
~ Mark Twain, author

Making the Decision to Homeschool
~ Mark and Helen Hegener

Do you remember when you first came across the idea of homeschooling your children? Did it just seem like a naturally good idea to you, or did you have to think about it for a while, try it on for size, find out more information about what might be involved, discuss it with a few people like your husband or your mother or your best friend, maybe even read a book or two on the subject in order to really warm up to the idea?

Did the thoughts of teaching your own children fascinate you—or scare you? Did you envision you and your kids sharing mornings filled with reading, crafts, gardening, baking, music-making and afternoons filled with explorations, discoveries, enlightenments and joy? Or did you wonder how on earth you could ever teach them chemistry or algebra, while envisioning a long, nightmarish struggle, more akin to your childhood homework assignments thrown at you all over again?

There are some people who can honestly say they took to homeschooling as a duck takes to water, but for the majority of parents, the decision probably came only after a lengthy exploration of what's involved. For many it came even harder, with long, agonizing nights of wondering if it was the right thing to do, heartfelt and sometimes heated discussions with family and friends, hours of poring over articles and books and magazines, searching for answers to their questions. Some parents started right out with optimism and high hopes, but too many others—most often the fathers—agreed to homeschooling only resignedly, half- heartedly, willing to try it, but just as willing to throw in the towel and send their kids to school at the first sign of difficulty.

Why is something so obviously good for parents and children so often approached with caution and concern? Why are some people so afraid of trusting their own feelings—their own good instincts—without validation from other people and most often from the so-called experts?

We were involved with an online discussion group among several friends for a few years, and this very question once gave us all an opportunity to share our thoughts with each other. We had saved much of this particular thread of discussion as inspiration for our own writing, but in re-reading our friends' contributions, we were struck by the power and eloquence of their writings, and we'd like to share them with you verbatim.

A close friend, Kathleen, wrote, "My point of view is simply that the system—whether you want to call that our government, or our school system or something else—has somehow taken away our basic human right to confidence in ourselves and acceptance of ourselves. When we equate 'all-rightness' with being like someone else, dissatisfaction and anxiety prevail. The product of those two are lowered self-esteem and inertia (unwilling to try for fear of 'failure'.)

"Adults are afraid to do everything. They rely on experts to doctor them, teach them, govern them, religion them. It is no wonder why they are anxious about homeschooling. They have no confidence or self-esteem themselves. Making mistakes is how people learn. We have to err to learn. Yet when we err, we cringe in fear and develop anxiety. I have come to know that not knowing something is no reason for anxiety. It is an opportunity to err gloriously."

One has to wonder why so many of us have lost our confidence—does it serve some greater purpose to have a complaint, pliable populations, or is it merely a byproduct, an unfortunate happenstance?

Another friend, Deborah, shared thoughts which really struck home for us as publishers. "While I don't know how people develop confidence and courage in this culture, I do know that they won't ever get it from publications that promise 'The Answers.' One thing I've noticed in all my favorite magazines (all subjects, not just homeschooling) is that they ask more questions than they answer. There's a sense of a shared journey, traveler's tales on the road, instead of a leader shouting back directions to those behind. 'This is what we do' has a different attitude about it than 'This is what everyone should do.' Ideas instead of Rules. 'Why we love math' instead of 'Ten tricks every math teacher should know.'

Deborah's words also touched a chord in our friend Marylee. "I really like what Deborah says about 'shared journey.' When I was so anxious my first year homeschooling, I sought out 'experts' (and I mostly mean 'old timers' who radiated confidence and common sense) to tell me things like 'trust yourself,' 'you know your kid and her needs better than anyone else,' 'trial and error is fine,' etc. I read as widely as I could, so that I could saturate myself with these thoughts, hoping to contain my anxiety. One of the main comforting messages that first year from the 'experts' was that anxiety was perfectly normal and would gradually fade as I developed more confidence. This helped me to remember that something only needs courage if it is frightening. Now that I'm more confident, I don't think of it as courageous to be homeschooling, .but the first year I felt both more scared and more courageous."

The image of scared but courageous new homeschoolers seeking something different for their children is one every support group leader is familiar with. It does take a while to adjust to this strange new idea, to even learn what questions to ask. Our friend Suzanne writes that when she's answering new homeschoolers' questions, she doesn't discourage them from using a curriculum or prepared materials if it's obvious they really want to. She adds, "My first recommendation is always for them to let their children be for awhile and for the parents to use that time to get more familiar with relaxed homeschooling, interest-based learning, unschooling. Sometimes the school-thing is so ingrained, they just can't. They want someone to tell them what to do for a bit until they do get that confidence. I've seen their troubled faces when they come to a meeting and want to know how to teach 'x' and are met with our bright chorus of, "we don't teach, our children teach themselves, we unschool, it's easy, you don't need textbooks.' Maybe some of unschoolers sprang forth fully 'unned' from John Holt's head, but I suspect that many more of us are still finding our ways."

This takes us back to Deborah's observations of a sense of shared journey, and travelers' tales on the road. In our conversations, there were the inevitable allusions to homeschoolers as pioneers in education and family issues. We've always liked this analogy, as the pioneers had to be brave and courageous and confident souls, working together, supporting each other, blazing new trails, building foundations for those who would come later. Because those scared but courageous homeschool pioneers forged ahead, parents now have a wealth of support to draw from, but important questions still face us on the trail ahead. And the questions are changing even as we're finding answers. Homeschooling is changing, evolving and developing and the decisions you make for your family—the ways in which you choose to help your children learn—are part and parcel of that change.

Welcome to the adventure! Welcome to homeschooling!

Mark and Helen Hegener are the parents of five always-unschooled children, now grown, and these days they enjoy learning along with several grandchildren, while overseeing publication of *Home Education Magazine* and HEM Books. The extended Hegener family makes their home in Alaska, producing books and videos on the Alaskan sport of sled dog racing.

Chapter 2

How Did Homeschooling Begin —and Where is it Going?

"The aim of education should be to teach us rather how to think, than what to think—rather to improve our minds, so as to enable us to think for ourselves, than to load the memory with thoughts of other men."

~ Bill Beattie,
founder of Pathways Danbury for at-risk kids

The concepts discussed in this chapter will help you to decide if homeschooling is something that may or may not work in your family. Remember that the core of homeschooling is flexibility, so take this information and bend it to what works for you before you make a decision. Homeschooling is almost always an option if you learn to ignore your self-imposed limitations.

What qualifications do I need to homeschool?

You will need dedication, confidence, enthusiasm, compassion, caring, and a strong belief in the natural curiosity of your children and their inherent drive to learn. Is that it? Basically. It's normal for you to ask yourself if you need some kind of special teacher training, but the answer from almost all homeschooling parents is a resounding NO. Perhaps John Taylor Gatto, former Teacher of the Year, puts it best when he wrote in Linda Dobson's *The Homeschooling Book of Answers*, "Let me reverse that question. Can you teach your children if you do have teacher training, did well in it, and believe its precepts of scientific pedagogy, its psychological principles of child development, its habits of time management, behavioral control, text selection, sequencing, assessment and guidance? I don't think so."

Teacher training only takes a parent's natural instincts and tries to alter them to fit the public school model of how children should learn. Parents that have had this training often cite it as one of the biggest obstacles they had to get past before they could homeschool their children properly. The key to it all is to remember this: homeschooling is not about teaching; it is about learning.

How much time does homeschooling take or will I still have time to do anything else with my waking hours?

At the risk of sounding like a broken record, this depends on you. There is no right or wrong amount of time to spend on homeschooling. Most of it will depend on how you decide to structure your teaching, how old your children are, how many children you have and the individual personalities in the mixture. Unschoolers may say they do not spend any set time on actual teaching during a day, while structured homeschoolers may estimate three to four hours a day on the average.

Why do public school students spend six or more hours a day in the classroom? Much of their time is spent in unnecessary busy work, walking to and from classes, handing in or handing out papers, waiting for attendance and other activities that are not actually part of learning. They also are sharing the classroom, materials and teacher with 20 to 30 other students, rather than a sibling or two, so they have to wait to ask questions or get help. At home, as with a personal tutor, a child can learn faster and easier. Experts estimate that what takes two weeks to learn in a public school class takes two to three days in a one-on-one environment.

In homeschooling, you also have great flexibility with your time. If your child is a late or slow riser, for example, why teach in the morning? Wait until the afternoon when he or she is more alert. If you work in the afternoon, homeschool in the evening. Teach on the weekends instead of the weekdays—it is all up to you and your personal schedule.

Keep your expectations of yourself and your children somewhat realistic. Don't try to be Super Parent every day and accomplish so much that each night you are exhausted. Whenever I met a parent who proudly showed me his or her hourly schedule for each day of the week, with all of the hours filled in with "learning experiences," I knew I was also most likely seeing a future burned out homeschooler. Please, take it easy, enjoy the time instead of feeling rushed to do more than is humanly reasonable.

Lastly, it is vital that you recognize that children are learning all the time. They do not need to have a workbook in their hands to be learning. They do not need you to be talking to them or explaining something to them to be learning. They can be outside playing in mud puddles and watching earthworms. They can be talking to grandparents on the phone. They can be figuring out how to put together a 1000-piece puzzle. All of these are learning activities. When you realize this, you can see that homeschooling doesn't have to take up all of your time at all.

How much does homeschooling cost?

It may sound like the type of vague answer you would expect from a politician, but it's the truth: it costs as much as you want it to. You can go to a teacher's supply store and spend hundreds of dollars on materials, or you can hit the library and the local garage sales and swap meets. Most parents do a combination, depending on their style of teaching and their budget.

According to recent research from the National Association of Independent Schools, the average tuition for private school in 2005-2006 was close to $14,000 for grades 1 to 3, $15,000 for grades 6 to 8 and $16,600 for grades 9 to 12. According to a report from The Frasier Institute and published in October 2007, the average public school costs $9.600 per child. Compared to these figures, homeschooling costs little. The average homeschooling family spends less than $4000 on each child each year and often much less than that. As Claudia Hepburn, co-author of *Home Schooling: From the Extreme to the Mainstream* put it, "...(homeschooling) has proven to be a successful and relatively inexpensive educational alternative. It merits the respect of policy makers, the attention of researchers and the consideration of parents."

New homeschoolers tend to spend the most (you will probably spend more in the first year than in the next few put together!). The more structured your homeschooling is, the more supplies and materials you will need. The main things that you will spend money on for homeschooling are:

- textbooks
- workbooks
- packaged curricula
- field trips
- homeschooling books
- magazine and newsletter subscriptions
- memberships to museums, zoos, etc.
- private lessons or tutors
- homeschooling conferences
- dues
- equipment
- computers and software
- manipulatives
- art supplies
- CDs and DVDs
- games

Again, not all of these things are absolutely necessary. Too often, new homeschoolers are tempted into spending hundreds of dollars on materials that end up sitting on a shelf unused because as colorful and wonderful as they looked in the store, they did not appeal to the children. Restrain yourself from going overboard on materials and wait to see what your kids enjoy—and what they do not.

How can you keep the cost of homeschooling down? Avoid those teacher supply stores that sell the new, expensive stuff and instead check out these possibilities for supplies:
- libraries
- garage sales
- discount bookstores
- thrift stores
- homeschooling curricula fairs
- homeschooling swaps
- schools
- used bookstores
- flea markets
- ebay and other online auctions
- other homeschoolers
- estate sales
- craigslist (a national online site for buying and selling)

Ask relatives to pay for your memberships or dues for your birthday; ask for gift certificates to your favorite suppliers for Christmas. Many families make their own manipulatives and write their own lessons to save money. Also, remember that by homeschooling, you don't have to pay for school lunches, new wardrobes, book rental fees, or transportation costs to and from school. If you really work on it, you may find that homeschooling saves you money!

What about socialization?

Without a doubt, this seems to be the main question that homeschoolers hear and almost all of them shake their heads and wonder why. Of all the concerns that one can come up with regarding homeschooling, the issue of socialization is among the smallest to worry about.

First, ask yourself just what your personal definition of socialization is. What most people mean is, will my children know how to get along with other people if they don't go to school? Will they know how to communicate and be polite? The answer is, unless you lock them in a closet and refuse to communicate with them, of course they will. To think otherwise means that you may well have a skewed perspective on the socializing that goes on in public schools and home schools.

The ability to socialize well with others implies that you know how to talk with people of all ages, types and backgrounds; how to convey your thoughts clearly; how to have your own individual thoughts and opinions that you can comfortably share with others; and how to listen to the thoughts of others in turn. Most of this does not happen in public schools.

Instead of being surrounded by people of all different makeups, children spend almost all their time with kids their same age. This is certainly unnatural and nothing like the "real world" where adults commonly interact with people younger and older than themselves. Instead of being able to talk freely, children in class are usually told to stay quiet and quit talking. How many teachers have said, "Quiet! School is not the place to socialize!"

By spending almost all of their schools hours with children of the same age, kids find themselves becoming peer dependent (I need to ask Susan if this outfit looks good; Jamie told me to stop acting so stupid at lunch), competitive (I have to do better than them or I won't make the team) and pressured (everyone else is trying pot and if I don't, they will think I am weird and won't like me anymore). They may find themselves labeled (geek, nerd, queer, lame, loser, suck up) and if they are unfortunate enough not to be among the elite group that is deemed popular, they may suffer from self-image and self-esteem problems. Is this the socialization you are afraid your children are missing out on? Is that what you want for your kids? Or, as John Holt writes in one of his books, "If there was no other reason for wanting to keep kids out of school, the social life would be reason enough."

On the other hand, in homeschooling, children are truly out in that "real world" they hear about in public school. They run errands with their parents, go to church, join 4H, Boy Scouts, Girl Scouts, the YM/YWCA, interact with other homeschoolers in support groups, play and talk with neighbors, take volunteer jobs, play on a community sports team, visit relatives, get a part time job, hang out at the library, and enroll in a wide variety of classes. They meet with people of all ages and types and even a trip to the grocery store can turn into a social event. "We never go anywhere that my children aren't talking other people," says one mother. "They talk to people in line, they ask questions of the clerk in the produce department; they chat with the check out girl and help the bagger load the groceries. Anyone who thinks that homeschooled children aren't social has never encountered my kids!"

If you are asking if homeschooled children get the same socialization that public schooled children do, the answer is a very emphatic no, they certainly do not. And it is for this reason alone that many families choose the homeschooling option in the first place.

What do I do if my child is already in school and I want to start homeschooling?

To withdraw your child from school is usually a simple process. Often it will depend on what state you live in. In some of the more open states, you do nothing. Other states require specific notifications. For the most part, even if you are in a state that doesn't require official notification, it is a good idea to contact your school so they know that your child is not truant and your child's teachers know not to expect him/her back in class. You can send a letter, call them, or stop in and tell them in person. Remember that no one knows your child or what is best for him/her better than you. Occasionally, you will encounter a public school official who smiles and wishes you all the best. Appreciate it. It's rather rare.

One step to take before you contact your school, however, is to talk long and deep with your child and spouse about this decision. Make sure that what you are doing is a unanimous decision. It doesn't look good to withdraw a child from school just to have Dad bring him/her back the next day—and it certainly does not make for harmonious family relationships!

How can we homeschool if we both work full time?

No matter what kind of homeschooling philosophy you choose to follow, it is going to necessitate some lifestyle changes. While the actual cost of homeschooling can be kept to a minimum, and time requirements are extremely variable, the daily routine of your household is going to be altered. If both you and your partner have full time jobs, this is especially true. Homeschooling is still possible, but it will mean you need to get creative. You won't be the only one out there looking for alternatives either. According to recent studies, more than 90 percent of working adults say they want to spend more time with their families and over 60 percent stated they would give up some of their pay for more time at home.

Here are some ideas to consider:

• *One of you quits.* Don't skip over this option until you give it at least a couple minutes of thought. How much is it costing you to work? What bills would disappear if you quit? Would it make that much of a difference in your income if you quit? If it would, is there a way to decrease other optional expenses like extra car payments, eating out, etc.? Homeschooling may indeed entail a financial sacrifice for your family, but consider the blessings and treasures that may come out of that sacrifice. Your children will only be young once; this might be the time to focus on being with them and leaving the pursuit of a career for later. How you decide which person is going to quit is up to you and your partner. Many parents base the decision on which person brings in the best income and/or has the best benefits.

• *Consider different working options.* Perhaps you can job share with another parent or alternate schedules with your partner. Some flexible employers will allow you to work your job flextime, meaning you have a different schedule than the traditional 9 to 5, but you still work a full 40 hour week. Other jobs offer the possibility of a compressed work week, where you still work full time but do in less than five days. You might also explore whether or not you and your partner can stagger your schedules so one of you is home most of the time.

• *Downsize your job to part time.* See if you can keep the job you have or something similar but go part time so you can be home more often or switch home times with your partner. Check also to see if you are eligible for early or gradual retirement from your company.

• *Develop a home business.* Do you have a skill, talent or hobby that can be profitable? Perhaps you are great handy-person, maybe you have knack for story telling. Take a close look at what you are good at and what you enjoy and brainstorm to see if there are ways to turn it into an income. Also, check with your employer to see if you could do part of your work from home. So much is computer-based these days that it just might be possible.

• *Take a telecommuting job.* Experts state that there are over 15 million people with telecommuting jobs today and they estimate that the number will rise to 50 million by the year 2030. There are several possibilities here, but watch out for scams because they are out there. Before you make a commitment of time or money, check with your local Better Business Bureau or the Federal Trade Commission to see what they have to say about the company. Some of the more known and trusted telecommuting business includes medical or legal transcriptionist, telemarketing, website designer, or in-home sales like Avon, Tupperware and Usborne Books.

I want you to know that when I write these ideas, I know that some of them are not easy. I also want you to know that I have been there, done that myself. When we had children and knew we wanted to homeschool them, I did not work outside the home. We gave up a second car. We stopped eating out. I took a lot of different jobs that I could do from home including selling Usborne Books and—of course—writing. We went without a lot of things for many years, but if I had to do it all over again, I would do it the same way.

Can I homeschool some of my children and have others in public school?

Yes, you can. Whether you will really want to is another question altogether.

Homeschooling one child and not another can create complications. Your kids may resent that you are handling their education in different manners (especially if they are teens and seem to be able to feel resentful if you say hello in the wrong tone of voice!). Give a lot of thought to why you have chosen these different options for your children. If you chose homeschooling for its flexibility and freedom, why wouldn't you want that for all of your kids? Don't be surprised if the child in public school starts to envy his or her sibling who isn't getting up, rushing for the bus and facing pop quizzes. If you choose this option, you will need to keep an open line of communication between you and your kids, as well as help them to keep openness between each other. Handle conflicts as they come up and be prepared for either one to want to try out what the other one is doing.

Can my child go homeschool part time and public school part time as well?

Yes, most public school systems will allow your homeschooled child to attend part time (but not all!). It may be called shared schooling, independent study, distance learning or dual enrollment. Check out the climate of your local school system; some are quite open to the homeschooling world and others are not. To make sure the school actually IS open to homeschoolers (as opposed to *saying* they are), go into the school with your child. How does it feel? For example, one of my favorite school stories happened with our eldest daughter. We lived just down the road from three schools and one day, she asked if she could go to the school's library and check out books. We were much closer to it than the public library, so we said we would check it out. We called and asked, and after weeks in which the school had to bring it up at a PTA meeting and get approval, they finally said yes. I walked in the first time with my daughter, and we went into the library. It was full of little desks and chairs and rows upon rows of books. After looking to see where some of her favorite authors were, I patted her on the shoulder and told her to enjoy herself and come home after she had picked out a few books. At this point, the librarian looked panicked and said, "Oh no. She is not allowed to sit down and read."

"Excuse me?"

"She can check out two books, but she cannot sit down and read in here."

"She cannot sit down in those chairs and read in a *library?*" (Catch the amazement in my voice?)

"No, that isn't allowed in here."

Well, what could I say to this idiocy? My daughter and I smiled at each other, rolled our eyes and went back home. There were other places to borrow books that came with a little more sanity built in.

Before you make the decision to let your child go to public school for a class or two, take a careful look at why you think this is the best option. Perhaps they just want to see what public school is like, especially if they have never been. After all, television and movies often make it look like a great place where the fun never ends. In this case, why not have them shadow another student for a day or two before making any kind of commitment? My oldest daughter did this in high school. After one day of shadowing a friend, she was more convinced than ever that public school was a complete waste of time. Sometimes school can look quite exciting and alluring to a homeschooler but once they see the reality of hall passes, limited bathroom trips, peer pressure and busy work, they may quickly change their minds.

Perhaps you are considering this option because schools can offer some opportunities that otherwise are hard to come by, such as choir, orchestra, drama, sports or driver education. Keep in mind that almost all these opportunities can be found elsewhere too. Look into your community for local organizations that would allow your child to explore these same options without having to get involved with the school. Community or church choirs, neighborhood or YM/YWCA sports teams, community theatres and orchestras and bands are available in most cities. Ask around. If you can't find one, don't despair—just start your own!

As for driver education, there are a number of options from online and correspondence courses, hiring a private company or just teaching your children yourself. In some states, this may mean they have to wait longer to get their driver's licenses but most parents feel that that is not such a bad thing. Some insurance companies offer discounts for kids who have taken driver education and gotten a good grade; check with yours to see if that also applies to homeschoolers.

Letting your homeschooler go to public school is an option that is open to you but shouldn't be entered into lightly. It can interrupt and complicate the flow of your homeschooling routine and it can involve your child in situations and behaviors that you have tried to avoid by homeschooling in the first place. It can undermine your confidence as he/she becomes involved in this different perspective on education—so think about it, talk about it with other homeschooling parents and with your children before you make any kind of commitment.

What if my child is doing well in public school?

Just because some children are successful in public school doesn't mean that it is a good or positive experience for them. There is, of course, the concept of "if it ain't broke, don't fix it." However, good grades should not be the only standard by which you measure if your children are doing well in school. While they have obviously learned to adapt to the inherent stresses and strains of traditional education, they can still be struggling in some areas. Perhaps they get straight A's, but have few friends; perhaps they are excelling in sports, but are bored in class.

If you considering homeschooling any of your children, please consider home- schooling all of your children. At the very least, offer each one the chance to try it. While children may seem completely satisfied in school, they may be even happier and more successful at home.

What if I am a single parent?

Yes, you can still homeschool, but like the couple that works full time, it may mean some lifestyle changes, and a good support system is essential. The primary complication for you will be what to do with your children when you are at work. How challenging this is depends greatly on their age and maturity. Older children can be left at home to take care of themselves and do independent work, while younger children cannot. You might check to see if you can bring them to work with you (nice, but rare); otherwise, you will need to arrange some kind of childcare. Choices here include family, friends and neighbors, as well as other homeschooling families. You might think about bartering childcare services or, if you aren't the babysitting type, barter a service that you could do in return. In other words, they watch your kids a few hours a day and you fix their cars, clean their houses, do their taxes, provide their dinners, etc.

A support group may be especially important for you. It can be your link to good sources of childcare, including a "mother's helper" type teen who loves kids and could use some extra income. Without a partner to discuss ideas, concerns and questions, the support group becomes vital.

Homeschooling can be a real issue in a divorce situation. If one spouse is opposed to homeschooling and decides to make it a problem that reflects custody rights and/or child support, you may well have a real battle on your hands. It this is true for you, and it is heading to the court's arena, experts recommend that you make sure you are complying with all the homeschooling laws in your state and that you provide high quality information about homeschooling's benefits to your attorney so he/she is able to go to battle forearmed with accurate and persuasive material.

Do moms do all the teaching or do dads have a role too?

The honest truth is that moms do the majority of the homeschooling simply because they are at home, on the average, for more hours than fathers. This is even truer in families that choose the more structured or traditional way of schooling. However, this doesn't mean that Dad doesn't have a role in the process. On the contrary, dads are often a very integral factor in whether homeschooling works for a family or not.

Most often, Dad's major role is as support person. Of course, there are families where this is not true—mine being one. Since we moved to Oregon six years ago, I have been the breadwinner (albeit upstairs in my robe at the computer) and my hubby has stayed at home to cook, clean and watch kids. Of course, none of them are babies or toddlers now, so he escaped the diaper/toilet training days, lucky guy. But he is the one at the kitchen table now, working on their spelling and coaching them along. I have to admit I miss it—those moments of learning together are precious. I am glad we were able to share it.

Besides the financial support a husband brings to the family, he can be a major support for his wife as she homeschools. He can listen to her concerns, and help her make decisions and figure out what directions to go and not go (these are officially known as homeschooling parent-teacher meetings!). He can support her in other ways as well, like helping with the household cleaning and cooking so her time is freer to spend with the kids. In addition to this, he can be a support to his children, listening to what they have learned, looking at their latest masterpieces and sharing his time and attention.

Along with this, there are a number of other ways dads can help. Here are a few ways they can be a part of the whole picture:
- Leading/teaching hands-on experiments
- Doing household chores
- Reading aloud
- Playing games
- Driving to and from field trips
- Sharing hobbies, skills, and personal interests with the kids
- Transporting to and from classes and activities
- Discussing what his kids are learning with his partner and contributing new ideas, thoughts and perspectives

- Picking up supplies, library materials, etc.
- Taking children to work with him to show them what he does

Many dads may think they are too busy to do much of this, but dads who want to be involved make the time, one way or another. Another influence on what role fathers play in homeschooling is the slowly growing number of stay-at-home dads across the country. According to the latest research, there are about 143,000 fathers staying at home with their kids while mom goes to work; 20 percent of fathers were the primary caregivers for their young children, and 32 percent worked evening shifts so they could be home with kids while mom worked during the day. For these men, their role in homeschooling will be far higher as they find themselves with the time and opportunity to do what they want.

"We are students of words: we are shut up in schools and colleges and recitation-rooms for 10 or 15 years and come out at last with a bag of wind, a memory of words and do not know a thing."
~ Ralph Waldo Emerson, poet

In the Trenches:

On Being a Homeschooling Dad

The first and foremost part of successful homeschooling is a positive attitude. Teaching is something that everybody does. Understanding the subject is crucial, but being able to reduce complicated factual relationships to the level of the student is the essence of teaching. Because parents are potentially capable of understanding their children like no one else on the planet, their ability to teach can easily surpass anything found in a public school.

Realize that your perspective is unique and therefore is necessarily different than a mother's. This means when you cover the same subject, your child has an entirely different teacher, a kind of two-for-the-price-of-one package. Blending these two perspectives makes for a truly superior academic approach. You will have areas of expertise, and you need to stand ready to add it when your wife's level of understanding tapers off.

Don't be intimidated by professionals who suggest that a child's learning progresses at a steady rate. Understanding and learning comes in leaps, jumps, hops, steps and the occasional stumble and fall. The child's effort to learn is much more important than actual measured achievement. This is true throughout a human's entire life.

A father forms the primary emotional cushion for the mother who may sometimes feel as if the entire educational process is her personal sentence for crimes not understood. He is there when she feels that if the multiplication tables or the recognition of nouns is not accomplished this day by this hour, her child will un- doubtedly fail at life, causing her to be ridiculed on national television. Intimate and personal communication between you and your wife is imperative—as are strategically planned meals out, and a backrub now and then. Homeschooling can be a hard row to hoe, but the rewards are many and so significant.

Gary, father of four, Indiana

My wife and I have four children and they have always been homeschooled. I have to say that the experience has taught me far more lessons than I could have ever imagined.

Lesson #1

Homeschooling allows me to be with my children far more than I would ever have been if they were in public school. I believe that giving my kids this time and attention will, at some level, help them to recognize that they are worthwhile people. Also, by being with them and listening to their responses and reactions, I learn more about their thoughts, concerns, desires and how they each process their world and its information.

Lesson #2

I am currently a househusband and I am learning more about running a house and the time it takes. I have a new understanding of how homeschooling can sometimes take the time that might have been spent on chores. Since I started staying at home, I have wondered what our culture thinks of men like myself at home while their wives earn the family income. The women I have spoken to are usually positive; the men I'm not so sure about.

I am slowly learning to take care of things like the laundry, meals, shopping and getting the kids to wherever they need to go on any given day (the older they get, the longer the list gets!). Yet I am still aware that despite this role reversal, my wife is still doing more housework than I was when I was the primary income earner and she was the one home with the kids.

Lesson #3

I am learning about myself through my children. I often see and hear myself within their childlike, innocent questions. As I struggle with them on something, I become more aware of my own ability—or lack of it—to be patient or my own habits and irritations. I flashback to the feeling of being in school and the frustrations it brought to me, and once again, I realize how much of what I had to learn in school was pretty stupid. Why in the world should anybody have to learn how to diagram sentences? Isn't it just better if they learn how to write, talk and communicate well? Why do they need to know what the parts are called if they are already using them daily, often on a brilliant level?

Lesson #4

Homeschooling has shown me that there comes a time when you, as the parent, have to know when to stop. When I am working with my 11-year-old son and I see the interest fade away, I often have to battle my own inner tapes on what to do next. Should I just let it go and start again later? This conflicts with the lessons in my head that tell me we should just finish what we started. However, I am coming to recognize that when the light goes out of my children's faces, it's time to go and do something else like go toss the ball, walk the dog, mow the lawn or weed the garden—all of them other possibilities to learn.

Lesson #5

I have come to recognize through the time I spend with each child how tremendously different each one is. My youngest son, for example, showed an early interest in reading and math, while his older brother showed very little. His interest is in the physical world, not the abstract. He wants to put things together and take them apart again. He wants to look at his pocketknife collection. He wants to look at girls and pretend that he isn't. Our two daughters are even more extreme; they certainly have approached the world with different styles, attitudes and pace.

Lesson #6
One of the most surprising lessons I have had is that children are learning all the time, not just when you think they are. My oldest son used to listen to my wife read each night and to all appearances, he didn't seem to hear a word she said. He was coloring, building with Legos®, moving his toys around. However, she and I were both amazed to find out he absorbed as much, if not more, than the others who were sitting still. His learning was obviously tied into motion itself. In school, would this have meant a label of ADD or ADHD? At home, it was just his way of learning.

Lesson #7
Relatives can certainly give you their opinions of homeschooling when they really know little to nothing about it. Are they truly concerned about the education and well being of our children, or are they angry because they had to go to school? Maybe they are just thinking that since we chose to homeschool, we are indirectly stating that they made the wrong decision with their children for putting them in public school. Perhaps the negativity comes from their own secret wish that they too had been homeschooled.

Lesson #8
I have come to wonder if perhaps the process of having and raising children is actually a natural part of our own personal maturation as adults. I know it has been a large part of mine. If we, as a society, abdicate a large part of raising children to others, don't we also stand a chance of stunting our growth?

Lesson #9
When my children are all grown up and have moved away, I am sure I will wish I could have them back for a little while. Without a doubt, I know I will be glad they spent most of their days at home with me and my wife, rather than sitting in school away from us.

Lesson #10
I have come to believe that one of the greatest ways to protect a child for the future is through homeschooling. I know that there is little research available on how homeschoolers fare in society (emotional problems, violent crime, drug and alcohol abuse, divorce, etc.) but I have to wonder, if it was done, what it would show.

Lesson #11

I have learned that the public school system teaches all of us that we cannot trust or have faith in ourselves and our children to have the internal, inborn wisdom to make the right choices or to learn what is important on our own. They are wrong.

Lesson #12

Lastly, as I spend time talking and being with my children, I am often completely amazed at the knowledge that they have, and I have absolutely no idea where it came from. What a delight!

Joseph, father of four, Oregon

In the Trenches
Socialization—Our Biggest Gripe with Homeschooling
~ John Andersen

Yes, socialization has been a huge problem for our children, but with experience, we have learned to bring it largely under control.

You see, we live in Portland, Oregon. Before we moved here, we suspected it was a good place to homeschool. Talk about an understatement! Everywhere we go, we run into homeschoolers. We have associations with dozens of homeschooling families. Without exception, they are all involved in a variety of activities. There are homeschooled roller skating parties, archery lessons, basketball group, high school band, community college courses, co-op language classes, volunteer opportunities, daytime art classes, music classes, singing groups, theatre productions, science labs at a local museum, organized field trips, Girl and Boy Scouts—the list goes on and on.

And that is the core of our children's socialization problem: too many activities and too little time.

Homeschoolers, without the constraints of a six-hour school schedule, are extremely vulnerable to falling into the trap of too many outside activities and too much social interaction. This can be dangerous, especially if we hope to teach our children to appreciate and enjoy the quiet, reflective life.

So, my wife Mandy and I are learning to apply the brakes, to slow things down a bit. One step we've taken is to develop a weekly schedule of sorts. We don't hold hard and fast to it but rather use it as a guide. It looks something like this:

Monday - At-home academically-oriented day; also clean-the-house day. Our children usually spend the late afternoon and early evening outside playing with the neighborhood children.

Tuesday - Co-op learning with other homeschoolers, also some academics and afternoon outside play with neighborhood children.

Wednesday - Mandy and children volunteer at the library. At the moment, they shelve books, label items and help with other projects. We try to do some academics as well and, of course, there is time for afternoon play outside again.

Thursday - Slow day (intentionally); sometimes co-op classes, evening achievement group for our daughter and Cub Scouts for our son.

Friday - Family outing day; this can be a volunteer project which we do as a family or going to the beach, visiting historic sites, the zoo, public gardens, museums, etc.

This general plan helps us to pace ourselves throughout the week and provides a "first line defense" against the constant barrage of social activities. It gives us a sensible framework and enables us to enjoy unhurried time together on a daily basis.

If you're thinking about homeschooling and you live in a city with tons of homeschoolers or lots of interesting things to do, you will definitely need to come up with a strategy to keep the socialization problem under control!

In the Trenches
Homeschooling and the Single Parent ~ Leanne Coffman

Being a single parent for the past three years has been a process of adaptation for me in many ways, especially with homeschooling. The demand on time and the individual attention both to academics and personality can be somewhat overwhelming even in a two-parent household, but for a single parent like myself, the process can seem truly daunting. I have found that flexibility and a less structured environment are vital to success. As a mother of three homeschooled children, I struggled initially with the pressure of being the sole breadwinner as well as with the responsibility for the upkeep of a home, the maintenance on the vehicle, the grocery shopping, the cooking, and the myriad other things that required my attention, in addition to the education of my children. At first, my thought was to succumb to the pleas of so many well meaning family members and friends who implored me to place them in public school. However, one of the greatest joys in my life has always been to teach my kids, to watch their eyes light up as they discovered the love of reading, or mastered some concept that they previously couldn't grasp. Additionally, my children had undergone much transition in their lives through our divorce, and I felt that they needed as much security and consistency as possible. One of the best ways I felt I could provide that was to continue to homeschool.

A typical day though, was now less than typical, due to errands, doctor's visits, my career, and my own continuing college education. I began reevaluating what my goals were with each child and what their specific, individual needs were. Prior to my divorce, I was extremely structured, using a grade-based system, and a certain amount of time per day deemed as "school time." As I reflected on what I was trying to achieve with my children and the lack of a consistent block of time for schooling purposes, I began to realize that education need not be appropriate to set periods of the day. Learning could instead be incorporated into our lives throughout the day. So using this approach, I began what I call "learning-as-we-go-lifestyle teaching." When we go to the grocery store, my children mentally add up the purchases, and we play estimating games to see who can come the closest to the actual price. When my early bird child comes to snuggle with me in the morning, often we spend our "cuddle time" reading a book. My older child and her sister take turns quizzing each other with math flash cards; the eleven-year-old learns her multiplication and division and the younger masters addition and subtraction. This is a good review for previously mastered concepts with the older child, and somewhat paves the way for the younger one to grasp math concepts that she hasn't technically learned yet. The baby of the family, currently age six, picks up on this and is frequently part of the action, surprising us with her unexpected ability to know the correct answer to math facts that many six-year-olds do not.

In finding an art teacher for my children, I was able to schedule some much-needed time for myself. Often I use this hour of free time to have lunch with a friend or to catch up on a project that I need quiet time for. When we take trips, (the most recent, a camping trip out West), we use the time to learn about nature and geology and American history. My children came home from vacation with priceless journals replete with drawings and stories of much learning and family times. Doctor's visits, errands, and car time find us using this approach as we cart our notebooks and flash cards and reading material with us. Audiotapes of famous people, great Americans, and sing-along states-and-capitals play in our vehicle as we scurry from place to place. Instead of using textbooks for reading, as I previously had, I began to incorporate the whole book approach. Now my older child and I take turns reading quality literature aloud to the other two. Spelling and vocabulary words come from our reading. Handwriting has taken on the format of writing letters to family and friends that we often, in our structured lifestyle, neglected. My own love of art and music has been passed on to the children as we use some of our family time to explore art museums or listen to different types of music as we do our housework. My eleven-year-old shares my passion for classical music and opera, while my nine-year-old enjoys blues. Cooking together has provided lessons in math, economics, and the ever-important ability to follow directions. The older girls cook lunch most days, sometimes surprising me with their creations (although we have had a few inedible episodes!) Care of pets and the process of doing their own laundry has taught all my kids valuable lessons in responsibility and has freed me up from tasks that used to require my attention.

While I still feel the demands from time to time of single parenthood, using the approach of homeschooling as a lifestyle and being flexible has given me back the joy of home teaching. When I look at my children, I feel good that the quality of their education has not suffered and perhaps has even been enhanced throughout this experience. The greatest affirmation of this came to me recently when my nine-year-old wrote a story about things that she was thankful for. The heading of the story was titled, "My Mommy and My Teacher."

The Voices of Experience

School through Another Lens:
Some Implications of Homeschooling
~ Patrick Farenga, Holt Associates

When we discuss how to improve education, it is so often a discussion that takes place within the confines of our ideas about conventional schooling: school is simply a vehicle in need of a souped-up engine (higher standards), a more comfortable interior (better facilities) or better instructors and testing instruments. Many parents who homeschool or send their children to private school feel they have purchased or built better cars for their children's education. However there are some, such as myself, who feel the automobile is going the way of the horse and buggy and that education is more than a race towards a degree that not everyone can win. By viewing the technology and rationale for schooling as outdated rather than in need of an update, we can see new types of vehicles to use or create and new paths to follow to help our children learn and grow.

For instance, if you judge education by counting degrees granted by education institutions, America is more educated than ever—more people hold college degrees in the U.S. now than at any point in American history. Yet we are seeing many college graduates not send their children to school for their education. A study by the U.S. Dept. of Education, "Homeschooling in the United States, 1999," notes that 25 percent of homeschool parents attained a bachelor's degree compared to 16 percent of non-homeschoolers; 22 percent of homeschooled parents have graduate/professional school degrees compared to 16 percent of non-homeschooled parents. Why are increasing numbers of people who have spent most of their youth in school and gone on to higher education, not sending their kids to school?

Researchers study the reasons why parents homeschool—quality of education, religious and poor learning environment in school are often cited—but to my knowledge, no one has explored exactly why so many college graduates homeschool their children . Perhaps it is for the same reason my wife and I decided to homeschool: we did not want our children to waste their time in the same empty rituals of education that we did. Passing tests only to forget the subject matter when the grades were given; spending years in foreign language instruction and passing the courses, yet being unable to have even a rudimentary conversation in the language outside of the classroom; struggling to learn advanced math skills that were seldom used outside of class; doing lab experiments that were more role exercises than explorations of scientific inquiry. Time and youth cannot be regained, and therefore, perhaps the real crisis in education may be one of disillusionment, among graduates rather than poor performance among current students.

One implication of the increase in homeschooling among college graduates is that the conventional K – 12 curricula are not considered by them to be vital to college admission or to finding work worth doing. The entire sequence of elementary, middle and high school is turned on its head or simply sidestepped by many homeschoolers. For instance, many high school age homeschoolers I know take community college courses instead of high school courses. When I was in high school, community college was considered a next level, not a substitute for high school classes. Whether homeschoolers use the classical *Trivium* or *Trivial Pursuit*, correspondence school or home-made curricula to help their children learn, the point is that a wide variety of methods and schedules are used successfully by homeschooling families. By examining how and why homeschoolers can do things differently than schools, we can see new directions for school and our general social good.

Homeschoolers will no doubt argue with some of what follows, probably on grounds of politics, individual freedom, or ideology. But my point is, regardless of these concerns, the actions I describe in this essay are nonetheless happening and we should be exploring them rather than ignoring them. What I describe are not theoretical constructs, but actual occurrences that we can duplicate, expand, adapt, or simply catch the spirit of.

Smaller Class Sizes

The costs of training additional teachers, building new classrooms and other expenses involved in reducing class size the way school officials want it done are immense. But there is an inexpensive baby-step that schools could take in this direction that would take very little effort on their part: encourage parents who wish to homeschool to do so. Parents help reduce public and private school class size when they decide to homeschool full time and there are probably other parents willing to teach their own kids just a few hours a week in certain subjects, thereby freeing the classroom teacher to work more intensively with those students who need him or her most.

Not everyone can or wants to homeschool, so there need not be worries that if schools openly view homeschooling as a complement to their efforts, rather than a threat, there will be a mass exodus from schools. There were roughly 50 million students, ages 5-17 in America in 2003; of those 1.1 million were estimated to be homeschooled. This is just 2.2% of the school age population, but what other program, at so little cost, achieves this same reduction in class size so easily, and with the willing cooperation of the families involved? Rather than fighting homeschoolers and parents seeking more one-on-one attention for their children, schools should be working with both groups as one small, cost-effective step towards reducing class size in America.

Computers and Distance Learning

One reason why more people are homeschooling today is because more materials and opportunities are available for learning at home than ever before. Curricula, support, mentoring, courses and texts are now as available at your average homeschooling conferences as they are at a professional teacher's conference. But the Internet has added a new dimension to this, and homeschoolers have taken to it much better than schools have. Homeschooling families are among the most Internet-savvy families today and snail-mail correspondence programs that flourished in the 80s and early 90s have readily morphed into on-line ventures. Further, families that that design their own curriculum find the Internet a valuable and inexpensive research tool: for instance, there is a book entitled *Homeschool Your Child for Free* that describes over 1,200 Internet resources for homeschoolers.

I have serious reservations about dedicating your homeschooling to learning via computer, but the point I want to make is that if you want your children to learn about computers and technology, then school isn't the best place for them. Dr. Larry Cuban, author of *Oversold and Underused: Computers in the Classroom*, notes that, "despite nearly $8 billion dollars spent annually on school technologies, the results get a failing grade . . . And when application is examined this powerful technology ends up being used in classrooms most often for word processing and low-end functions that maintain rather than alter teaching practices. The promise of a technological revolution in our schools remains largely unfulfilled."

The free form, non-linear aspects of on-line searches and communications, and the very dedicated role-playing and strategy games are particularly interesting to many of the homeschooled children I talk to who use computers as part of their schooling. I think schools and computer visionaries would be wise to study how and why computers are used in homeschools instead of spending more time and money seeking ways to push conventional school content and methods over the phone lines.

On-line tutorials, email critiques of writing, serious research, social interactions and the development of new teaching strategies because of the computer are flourishing in the homeschool arena. Further, this is happening among families of modest means. Homeschooling is not primarily taking place among wealthy families who can afford the best computers and expensive on-line services; the 1999 Federal study of homeschooling showed that the average household income of homeschoolers was no different than non-homeschoolers.

Other Places for Kids to Be

Sometimes neither school nor homeschool is the right place for a child to be, but where else can they go, who else can they be with, during school hours? John Holt wrote a lot about this topic, particularly in his book *Instead of Education: Ways to Help People Do Things Better.* Another visionary in the education without schools movement is Don Glines, director or Educational Futures Projects. Glines was an advisor for a lifelong learning system without schools or schooling for the proposed Minnesota Experimental City, a project that almost took flight in the 70s. There are a few alternative programs and schools that attempt to make the world more accessible for children during school hours, but homeschooling puts even more flesh to the bones of these ideas today, such as:

- *Studying or playing in other people's homes.* Homeschooling cooperatives continue to flourish as more people homeschool and pool resources.
- *Working alongside adults and professionals in safe environments.* Volunteerism, internships, apprenticeships and helping out in family businesses are among the many ways homeschoolers create knowledge, friends and opportunities outside of the home. Many children

learn skills better in real life situations than they do in abstract class situations. For instance, some children learn math better by making change at a yard sale or by building a bookcase than by doing problems in a textbook about making change or building a bookcase. Homeschoolers, and a few schools, have successfully had children of all ages spend school hours in volunteer or apprentice work situations in lieu of school attendance, not just as an after-school enrichment program.

- *Martial arts, language, cooking, hands-on science, computer and other types of specialized schools* can be open during school hours if children were allowed to be there in lieu of public school. Homeschooling is giving many of these new places new clientele during school hours, providing them with new revenue streams. Museums in Boston have set up courses and activities just for homeschoolers during times they aren't serving school groups.
- *Family resource groups.* Some are for-profit and are aimed at serving the homeschooling population during school hours; others serve any and all as afterschool programs.
- *Safe haven and financial security.* There is a need for safe places where children can go for shelter from the barrage of mass culture they encounter each day, as well as from abusive home or school situations. Areas set aside for peaceful reflection by children during school hours and access to people, funding and resources to help individual children and their families during school hours could benefit not only the personal lives of children but their academic lives as well.

Holt often noted that if we improve the general quality of life for people, we improve their education quality as well. These are just some of the sorts of places children can be other than home and school. Homeschoolers seek or create them out of necessity, but I think many other parents and children would welcome other safe places to go during school hours if they were allowed to use or create them.

Social Glue

We do need social glue, but I question if public school, as we have conceived it, is capable of producing this glue anymore. When Horace Mann and John Dewey put forth the concept of school as a common denominator for creating good citizens, providing a common set of civic and intellectual knowledge to a diverse, growing immigrant population, there were no radios, televisions, videotapes, DVDs, movies and the Internet. These, and so many other inventions and developments over the past hundred years compete with or usurp the common denominator role of school today. Certainly it can be argued that they provide an inferior product than schools, but their seductive power, ease of use and ubiquity make them very powerful competitors to school for creating social glue. Reevaluating how we use and perceive media and attempting to use them to help us create social glue is a discussion that only seems to happen in the realm of morality (too much sex and drugs on TV, misogynistic music, etc.) not in the realm of democracy, social integration and education. It is time we acknowledge that we are in a new century of learning and that many other institutions, people and influences deeply educate our children and society besides school.

Further, school has always been less about social interaction and democracy and more about direct instruction and grades. A homeschooling mother in New York City, Rita Sherman, wrote eloquently about the dilemma in 1923 in her book *A Mother's Letters to a Schoolmaster:*

"We, the State, for a hundred years, gathered our children together in a school, from all classes of society, upon a common ground, for a common purpose, and then have rested our case for a democratic education upon the self-satisfiedassumption that this democracy of intent is sufficient, evenfinal. We have allowed it to presuppose a democracy applied,practiced and produced!

We must be rid of this vanity. An honest analysis will show youthat the school as a democratic institution has progressed no farther than a decree of compulsory attendance."

Children are increasingly referred to by educators and politicians as resources to be exploited, whose test scores can raise property values or cause teachers to lose their jobs, rather than as individuals with particular needs and desires. Is it so hard to imagine that the violence that has been in our public schools for decades—think of the movies "Blackboard Jungle" from the 50s and "Dangerous Minds" from the 80s—and which is now brimming over into the public's view in the 90s with Columbine and its spawn, is at least partially related to the impersonal social sorting machine school has become?

The pressure our children face today is much worse than what we faced as children in school. Doriane Lambelet Coleman, author of *Fixing Columbine: The Challenge of Liberalism*, notes, "The nation's suicide rate increased 400 percent from 1950 to 1990. And even this extraordinary number was most recently reported to have doubled since 1990. "According to the Center for Disease Control and Prevention's Annual Summary of Vital Statistics, the suicide rate rose from 7.3 per 100,000 to 8.2 per 100,000 in only a year (2003 to 2004).

The gross incivility schools can have towards their students has been remarked upon for years by liberal critics of schools such as Ted Sizer (*The Children are Watching*) and by conservative critics such as Charles Silberman (*Crisis in the Classroom*), yet little has been done to make school society more civil. Pitting children against one another for the reward of grades and individual class standing and showing how much we value this competition by continually funding it over other less "educational" areas such as athletics, art, drama, extracurricular activities, volunteerism, community activism, or clubs sends a clear message to our children about what is really important to adults and our conception of "the social good."

Feeling good about ourselves and what we can do, respecting people who are different from us, working with people from different social classes and educational backgrounds, becoming a good citizen: I just don't see how school is supposed to accomplish these things by pitting student against student, school against school, district against district, in a race for higher test scores and property values. I find it striking how in our day and age, where you went to school classified you rather than equalized you!

John Holt noted that, "the important question, how can people learn to feel a stronger sense of kinship or common humanity with others who are different?" can not really be addressed by talking, preaching, discussing, bribing or threatening people in school. The answers, Holt wrote, come from people "who have enough love and respect for themselves and therefore have some left over for others."

I believe that integrating different people into a social whole is achieved best through group activities, teamwork, cooperative efforts and projects, games, conversation and sharing common goals, not by separating out the economic winners and losers of society based on tests taken in their youth and where their parents can afford to live.

Homeschooling shows that many parents support and create group activities as an integral part of their children's school day, not as extra-curricular activities. Often, as many classroom teachers as well as homeschoolers have written, the needs of children have little to do with the needs of the school curriculum.

These are but a few of the areas where I think homeschooling can shine new light on old assumptions about children and learning and show by its spirit and practical application, new ways of integrating children and adults for society's greater good.

Chapter 3

How Do I Get Started?

"Education would be much more effective if its purpose was to ensure that by the time they leave school every boy and girl should know how much they do not know and be imbued with a lifelong desire to know it."
~ William Haley, newspaper reporter

Once the decision is made that homeschooling is the right route to go, or at least try out, the next question is often, "What now?" This chapter gives you the information you need to know to start the journey.

Where can I get curricula to use?

Many new homeschoolers believe that they cannot begin until their desks are overflowing with textbooks and workbooks. While find the right curriculum is an important step for some; it is not necessarily the first step. To start, just sit back and watch your children: learn about them. What are their strengths? Weaknesses? What does he hate to do? What does she love? It is from these answers that parents can begin to choose the best curriculum.

Places to start looking include:
- Parenting magazines: look in the classifieds
- Homeschooling magazines: ignore the articles for a little while and read all of the classified and display ads
- Libraries: what does your community library have to offer homeschoolers?
- Catalogs: child development and educational catalogs will all offer wonderful things. Don't overlook toy catalogs too—they often include educational products.
- Newspapers: your local newspaper can have lots of helpful homeschooling material from learning to read with the comics, doing crossword or suduko puzzles, looking at sports scores and weather forecasts to just reading the articles and learning about the world.
- Other homeschoolers: ask them for what materials they did and did not like and why. See if you can look at what they have and even borrow some if possible. Try it out with your kids and see if they like—or don't.
- Your own home: You already have many of the things you need to get started right in your house. Younger children can learn lessons for months based on measuring cups, paper plates, glue, crayons, scissors, paint, cards and dominos. Check out your own bookshelves for good books to use.
- Other ideas: thrift stores, garage sales, teacher supply stores and curricula fairs.

Keep in mind when choosing any kind of curriculum that it is a trial and error process. You may try one company's workbooks and your son hates them while the one you got for a quarter at your neighbor's garage sale is his favorite. Before you invest a lot of money, get a good handle on what kind of materials your children relate to. Some kids love workbooks, and others run screaming into the night when they see one. Some kinds love hands-on experiments and manipulatives while others would be more content reading about them. Also consider what you like to work with because as the teacher, your opinion counts too.

Do I have to teach the same things/subjects that the public schools teach?

Have to? Absolutely not. Want to? Hope not. You may have some basic subjects that you have to cover in your state, but how you do it is up to you and you are only limited by your imagination. Who is to say that rock sorting isn't elementary math; a bike ride over the mountain trails isn't physical education or that cooking dinner for friends isn't home economics (not to mention a touch of math and health thrown in!)?

If you plan to homeschool a short time and then place your child back into public school (to cover a suspension/expulsion, to get through an illness or trauma, etc.), you might want to use the same textbooks and materials the school is using so he/she can merge back in easily. However, other than that, there is little reason to limit yourself to whatever the local school uses. In fact, there are compelling reasons not to! Their choices are not necessarily the best ones and certainly not the most interesting ones. Make better choices for your kids, and involve a mix of reading, discussing and experiencing in ways schools cannot begin to imitate.

Can I create my own curricula?

Yes and I hope you do so. While your state may have rigid requirements on what has to be taught, there are limitless ways to fulfill those requirements, and many of them can be created at home by you or by mixing and matching a wide variety of materials. Packaged curricula are often attractive to homeschoolers: they are convenient, and they are easy. Here, they say in their siren's song, just buy me and you won't have to give another moment's thought to any other materials you need for this entire grade/subject/child. However, more than a few of them will end up sitting unused and collecting dust or being donated to the thrift store because they just do not fit the learning style, interest of grade level of the child you bought it all for. A packaged curriculum is geared for the masses, not for the individual. As John Taylor Gatto bluntly puts it, "Nobody can develop a curriculum for you that isn't, at the very best, second best and, at the very worst, a rather diabolical exercise in mind control—even if its intentions are honorable."

How do I know which grade my child is in?

Does it truly matter? Really. Think about it. Why does that question matter outside of the public school system? Grades are something that schools assign to keep children of the same age herded together like sheep. Your child, being the human that he or she is, cannot possibly be the same level in all subjects. Are you? Are you as good in reading as you are in math? How well do you cook? How quickly can you convert Fahrenheit to Celsius and back again? How are you at running laps, speaking a foreign language or knowing the major imports and exports of Uganda? What grade level do you think you are in social studies, math, science, P.E., English, French and home economics? Do you think that other people YOUR age are better or worse than you? Uh oh. Maybe you're in the wrong grade.

The fact is that people all have strengths and weaknesses and that is how it should be. Perhaps your child is at the eighth grade level in age but reads at a fifth grade level and does college level trigonometry or the other way around. Toss out the concept of grades and just watch your children and see what ability they have in each subject area. If they are reading at 10th grade level, the fact that they are only nine doesn't matter. Buy reading material at the tenth grade level. Conversely, if they are doing fifth grade math and they're 18 months old, so be it. If they find themselves in a position where they need to know more math, they will learn it then. My oldest daughter got a job as a waitress. She learned more about basic math in one week on the job than she did in the previous two years. My second daughter volunteered at Habitat for Humanity. She suddenly had to learn fractions and percentages for building and measuring. It became important so they learned it.

Don't let yourself get stuck in the mindset of public school. Grade levels are just arbitrary levels that mean nothing to your developing, discovering child. Real life means you do well in some areas and not so well in others—unless you need to and then you improve. That is why one person is an accountant instead of a plumber or an attorney instead of a chef. Interests and abilities are what lead each person in the direction they want to go; grade levels have no relevance whatsoever. Toss that worry out the window now.

What does "deschooling" mean?

Have you heard how deep sea divers have to spend time decompressing before they can come up to the surface in order to prevent getting injured? Kids who have been removed from school to homeschool often have to spend time deschooling or they may risk emotional damage. When you bring a child home after they have been in school for any time, he or she needs time to adjust, to get used to this all-new lifestyle. Imagine if you worked a 40-hour week for years and suddenly you were able to stay home all day, everyday. It takes some getting used to!

How will your child react? It depends on your child's personality. One may sleep 14 hours a day, another might veg out in front of the television for all of her conscious hours. Some kids might follow you around like an extra shadow telling you "I'm bored . . . there's nothing to do . . ." while others may lock themselves in their rooms and not come out for a while. Let them! They need this time to acclimate, and pushing them to do anything educational can often result in anger, unhappiness or plain rebellion.

Think of an animal that has been caged up for most of its life. When the animal is suddenly set free, it often freezes in one position until it is convinced it is safe to move again. Your child may freeze in front of the computer, out on the back porch, or right next to you.

Please forget launching into any kind of curriculum for a while and let your child just 'be' for a bit, especially if his experience in school has been a traumatic one. Spend this time doing fun things together instead. Let your child explore time that isn't attached to bells and deadlines.

A number of homeschooling authors, parents and advocates believe that children need between six weeks and six months to decompress for every year spent in public school. Be patient; your child is like a caterpillar getting ready to emerge from a cocoon. Imagine what might be hiding inside!

What are learning styles?

Have you ever noticed that your child seems to process things in a totally different way than you do? Does she learn a song the first time she hears it or does he seem to ignore what you are explaining to him and then come back later knowing it perfectly? Dr. Howard Gardner, a psychologist at Harvard, may have an explanation for this.

Gardner did a great deal of research about how people think and process information, and he came up with the concept of multiple intelligences. Explained in detail in his book *Frames of Mind*, his philosophy is that people—including children—learn in eight distinct and different ways. How does this affect you as a homeschooler? Knowing what learning style works best for your children will help you immensely in selecting curriculum and planning activities, as well as give you a better understanding of why some teaching methods work miracles and others just go "splat." As the Lepperts wrote in their book, *Homeschooling Almanac*, "Learning styles is a philosophy that recognizes that we all perceive and process information in unique ways."

Read the descriptions of each type of intelligence listed below and consider which one(s) seem to fit your children and yourself the best:

- *Linguistic.* These people love words and love using them in all of their forms. They enjoy reading, they spell well and are typically great story- tellers. To learn best, they read the material or listen and take detailed notes. Fun activities for these learners include crossword puzzles and word searches.
- *Logical/mathematical*: These people see patterns in things; they love problem solving and can often take the abstract and turn it into reality. They enjoy doing logic puzzles, sudoku, sequencing and reasoning things out. Logical learners often turn out to be computer programmers, inventors or accountants.
- *Spatial/visual*: These people think and see things in images or pictures. They need to actually see what you are trying to tell them and do best with charts, graphs and maps. They make amazing

architects and artists.

• *Musical*: These people are almost always humming, singing, whistling or dancing. They express themselves best through music and are often aware of a sound's pitch and rhythm. They learn best if they hear the information put to music and may request a music tutor to teach them a variety of musical instruments.

• *Body/kinesthetic:* These people have just got to move to make life tolerable. They seem to be in constant motion, and they learn best from activities that are hands-on. They want to touch the materials and move them around. They may memorize facts while doing jumping jacks or running laps because it is through movement that they are able to process information the best. And yes, these are the children who are most likely to be diagnosed as ADD or ADHD. Instead of having a learning disability, many of them may just have a learning difference, and since schools are not able to cope with teaching in a kinesthetic manner (especially with 30 other learning styles in the same room to contend with!), this style becomes a problem—a problem that far too often results in a mind numbing drug that shuts down any of the normal learning processes of the child.

• *Interpersonal:* These outgoing people have the ability to bring others together. They enjoy other people and work best if they are with a partner or a group. They are sensitive to how individuals around them are feeling and often act as the peacemaker. Some may perceive them as too talkative or controlling, but these are the people who are never friendless and make fabulous leaders.

• *Intrapersonal:* These learners are often loners, preferring to spend a lot of their time in the complex workings of their own inner minds. They are introspective with a very high self-awareness. They tend to be rather bookish and independent; what some may take as aloofness is really just their style of relating to the rest of the world.

• *Naturalist*: These types are keenly aware of their environment. They enjoy spending time outside communing with and studying nature. They usually enjoy working with animals or plants and make terrific gardeners.

How do you know where your children fit into these different intelligences? Watch them closely. Where are their interests? What do they do when you give them new information? When they are deeply interested in something, how do they seem to learn the material? The answers to questions like these will give you clues to what blend of learning styles they use. Remember, of course, that just because one of your children happens to be a spatial learner, that doesn't mean any of your other children happen to be one. Just like one loves bananas and another can't stand them, children's learning styles are unique and personal.

One of the biggest perks of homeschooling is that you can support and adapt to each one of those specific learning styles as you need to. Instead of being in a situation where they are forced to learn in ways that feel difficult and frustrating, your children can learn in ways that are comfortable and natural. As the Lepperts put it, "Imagine putting 30 different people in one room and then wondering why they don't do things the same way, see things the same way, agree on everything and desire the same things. Yet this is exactly what is expected in mass schooling today."

What is the homeschooling continuum?

There are many different philosophies within homeschooling and they range from one extreme to another, thus making a sort of continuum. Where you and your family fall on this line is up to you and your attitudes about children and learning. Your memories of your own education will often send you in one direction, while watching your children on a daily basis may well send you in another.

I would hazard to bet that there is not a single homeschooling family on the planet that began homeschooling with one style and stuck to it all the way through. It is so much of a trial and error process that shifts with time, experience, children, successes and failures. What works for you might not work for your children; what works with the first child may not work with the others; what works great for the first year may feel wrong the next. This is an area that truly requires flexibility and open mindedness. It requires you, as the parent, to sit back and re-evaluate what is happening within your homeschool. Are you and the kids enjoying it or dreading it? Is it something that is a natural part of your life or something that is forced? Ask your kids. Is this working? What needs to change? What can we do differently to make it better for all of us?

As you read over the styles listed here, you may find one that sounds best to you overall, and that is most likely where you will start your homeschooling journey. As time passes, you will shift one direction or another as you listen to your inner feedback and your children's responses. Remember that if anyone in the homeschooling picture is miserable, something is wrong. For example, if you are trying to teach your children to read and he is ending up in tears as you mutter expletives under your breath, there is a problem that needs to be changed.

This happened with our first child. She was SIX so it was TIME TO READ. Within two weeks, neither of us wanted to touch a book—something we usually did with great pleasure several times a day. Fortunately, I was at least wise enough to realize a change was needed. I stopped teaching. She started learning.

I personally see this continuum as a long line and on the far left end is simply *traditional homeschooling*, also known as *school at home* or *structured homeschooling*. This philosophy is based on teaching the same material and using the same methods as the public school system. It can even go so far as to utilize report cards, tests, school desks, recess periods and bells. Families often choose this style with they first start homeschooling because if feels the most familiar to them. It represents what they think of when they hear the word "school." This method typically includes a packaged curriculum based on those old three R's: readin', writin' and 'rithmatic. It is quite structured with certain times of each day allotted for specific subjects. It is parent- or teacher-centered as the adult is the one in control of what will be learned, as well as when and how. While this method can work very well for some families, it also tends to be exhausting and can cause a lot of burn out for both parents and kids.

Next along this line is *classical home education*. Its focus is on developing critical thinking skills in children through a combination of teaching classic languages (Latin and Greek) and using a curriculum based on the 'great books' of Western civilization. The foundation for this method is known as the Trivium. Parents who follow this philosophy believe that children's cognitive development comes in three stages and that each one requires different materials.

The first stage is grammar (up to age 12), and this is when reading and writing are taught, as well as the skills of listening and observation. The second stage is logic (middle grades), and it brings in the abilities of in-depth and abstract thought. The last stage is rhetoric or wisdom (later teens), and this is where the child should be able to express his knowledge eloquently. This philosophy is not a common one, and the heavy emphasis on reading classics often makes it difficult for children to stick with.

Following this is Dr. Raymond and Dorothy Moore's philosophy of *delayed academics*. After years of research, this husband and wife team determined that most academics should not be taught to a child until at least age eight or 10 or even 12 because they are not truly able to competently understand and perform them before then. They also advocate strict schedules using a three-pronged approach to a balanced education: study on a daily basis, spend equal time in manual work of some kind and spend at least an hour a day doing some sort of home or community service. Much of what they base their recommendations on is Biblically based. Some parents find that the strict routines this philosophy calls for are too difficult for them to maintain.

Next is a homeschooling style based on the tenets of Charlotte Mason, an early 19th century British educator. It is often called the Living Books method as it places a very strong emphasis on having children read books that are lively and relevant to them rather than textbooks. Mason recommended a minimum of one hour a day on structured academics, followed by time out in nature exploring and observing. One of Mason's biggest concepts was the importance of reading out loud to a child and having him or her repeat the information back in a narrative style. She felt this helped childreen play an active part in learning information, as well as helping comprehension and listening skills.

As you approach the middle of the continuum, you arrive at the teaching philosophy of *unit studies*. Utilizing unit studies in your homeschooling plan means that you or your child (depending on where you fit between parent- centered and child-centered schooling) selects a subject of interest and you immerse yourselves in it for a month or more. The topic is looked at as a whole, not just as a history or science assignment. For instance, if you wanted to do a unit study on Egypt, you might go to the museum and talk about the mummifying process (science), look up some Egyptian recipes and try them at home (home economics), learn how to write your name in hieroglyphs (penmanship), get some books on Egypt from the library (reading), build a pyramid out of paper and glue (art), write a skit about King Tut and perform it (English/Drama) and go out to an Egyptian restaurant and talk to the people there (field trip). Unit studies are quite flexible and can be made part of the structured homeschooling schedule or all the way to the other end in the unschooling department. Since so much time is spent on one subject, kids can weary of it; letting them make some of the choices can make a real difference in keeping their interest.

The eclectic approach is probably the most popular method with veteran homeschoolers. Here you will find families using a little of everything in their homeschooling plans. They mix their packaged curriculum with what they have made themselves; they each select different topics to study; they spend time on their basic academics and a lot of time studying other things entirely. As Kathy Ishizuka wrote in *The Unofficial Guide to Homeschooling*, " . . . eclectics truly expound the smorgasbord approach to homeschooling. They pick and choose from the array of philosophies, teaching methods and curricula, employing whatever happens to work in their home at a particular time . . . eclectics make deliberate choices according to their children's nature and abilities." With this method, there is a great deal of flexibility, substantially decreasing the risk of burnout for both parents and children.

Finally, on that arbitrary far right of the continuum, there is the concept of *unschooling*, a term originally coined by educator, author and homeschooling forefather, John Holt over 40 years ago. Also known as *natural learning, child-led learning* or *interest-led learning*, it is as opposite of school as it can get. Instead of emulating or imitating the traditional method, it sheds those concepts and wants little to do with them at all.

In unschooling, the child is the one in control of what is learned when and how. Parents are not so much teachers as they are guides and mentors. They closely watch their children and help them to explore and learn about what they are already curious about. Unschoolers rarely utilize any kind of formal curriculum: they don't expect a child to follow a set timetable for when he or she learns something. Instead, these parents have a deep trust and respect in a child's inherent drive to learn, explore and discover. In return, they make sure to provide a very rich environment to learn in, with many materials and opportunities available to access on a daily basis. With unschooling, there is no coercion to learn because the child is at the helm of the direction his or her education is going. A child is allowed to learn in his or her own style and at his or her own pace rather than trying to match the style and pace of a teacher.

This method is very difficult for some people—even some other home- schoolers—to accept. It appears too easy, even negligent to some, yet it is the same method that was used to teach children how to walk, talk, get dressed, etc. Those lessons weren't taught or graded; they were modeled and assisted and they happened. Unschoolers believe this is true in all aspects of education.

For those children who have been in school for a year or more, this method may be difficult since they are used to being told what to do, when to do it and how to do it. That will improve, but it can be frustrating for parents and kids before it does. If you live in a state that requires documentation for what your children are doing, this method can be challenging since much of your children's activities will not clearly fall into one subject area or another. Mary Griffith wrote in her book, *The Unschooling Handbook*, "Unschooling parents who live where they must document their children's learning to comply with their state's legal requirements often devote considerable time and ingenuity to translating what their children do into terms that make sense for reports designed for a more conventional approach to education."

Whatever method you end up choosing to use with your children, be flexible. Homeschooling is a trial and error process as you discover what works and doesn't work for you and your children. Try it one way and if people aren't happy, change it. Experiment and find the right niche on the continuum; just don't be surprised if you're changing it again in the months to come.

Are state tests required? What do I do if they are?

Some states do require testing for those homeschoolers who are registered. (Whether or not you chose to register is a personal decision. There are those who feel that it is important to meet all of the state legalities. Others want their state to not even know they exist so they lie low.) If taking tests is part of your state's homeschooling requirements, prepare your child for taking them. You can do some practice tests as found in test preparation books online. Community colleges also offer test prep classes, so call them and see what they have lined up. Make sure you have covered all of the material that needs to be covered before taking the test and that you review it together. By taking a few trial tests, you can also pinpoint your child's weaker areas and spend some extra time on those before the test.

Make sure you know all the rules of the test; how and when it will be administered, who has the right to administer it, what will be done with the result and so on. One mother who had to have her child tested stated with a chuckle, "He has to take the test—but the results do not have to be mailed in or reviewed by anyone. So, we just take it for fun and to fulfill the silly requirement."

Check to see who has to administer the test. In some areas, there are homeschool parents who are former teachers who qualify to do this. They are often easier to work with because they understand your perspective and feelings. In other areas, the test can also be done in your home where your child is usually more comfortable.

Do not let yourself be fooled either—some public school administrators may try to tell you that you have to test your child when the law does not require it at all. Learn your state law, and then do not let anyone sway you on what has to be done.

How early or late can I start homeschooling?

The question of how early is simple: start the day your child is born. Every single day of a child's new life is a myriad of lessons. They are genetically driven to learn from you, so homeschooling starts at birth.

How late? There have been parents who have pulled their children out of school in their senior year of high school. There is no such thing as a time that is too late to homeschool. You do it whenever you perceive the need to be there. Nothing else matters.

Should I go year round or take the summers off?

Like so many other decisions, this is up to you. If you are following the same basic pattern as the public school, you may want to stop lessons for the summer. Others who unschool go all year round since they have never actually set class times and schedule. Many families opt for a mixture of philosophies; they teach formally during the typical school year and let up during the summer, focusing on more fun and relaxed lessons like field trips, vacations, experiments, etc.

Do I need to keep records/report cards/documentation of

what we do?

How much you need to do in this department will depend primarily on what style of homeschooling you follow and what your state regulations mandate. Some parents never write a single thing down while others maintain accurate and precise records on every child.

Here are the main types of record keeping that homeschoolers tend to use:

• *Journal:* This is written by the parents and/or the homeschooler and acts as a log, listing the projects done, books read, field trips taken, etc. It can be divided in any way the writer sees fit from separate sections for each child, day, subject, event and so on. This is probably the most casual, relaxed approach to record keeping.

• *Portfolio*: Compiled by either/both parents and kids, this is a multi-media record of what the homeschool year has encompassed. It can contain:

Poetry	Stories	Ticket stubs
Projects	Letters	Certificates
Rewards	Test results	Attendance records
Drawings	Art work	Photographs

A portfolio can be as casual or formal as you want it to be, and it is a great way to reflect the many different results your kids produce during their home- schooling adventure. Author Loretta Heuer, M.Ed. wrote in her book, *The Homeschooler's Guide to Portfolios and Transcripts*, "A portfolio is a collection of artifacts that has been selected from a larger body of work—a carefully designed sampler that is created for a specific reason. In essence, it is a portrait of you in a particular setting."

• *Schedule and subject log:* Modeled after public school teacher's daily logs, this has places to show what each child does each day, attendance, grades and other typical school information. These logs can be created at home or you can buy them at teachers' supply stores.

• *Transcripts:* These papers will list the titles of the courses your children take, as well as the credit hours and grades, just as public school transcripts do. These are certainly the most formal way of recording what you do and some families like them because they are easy to show to school officials, college interviewers and other people involved in education. Heuer writes, "A transcript . . . is like a snapshot. It gives the reviewer a quick look at you, your skills and your knowledge."

Whatever type of records you keep, remember that you will need to know how to take children's daily activities and figure out how to label them in educational-ese. Was the trip to grandma's house physical education (you took a long hike in the woods there), history (she told you all about her experience with rationing during World War II) or home economics (you helped her can her summer green beans)? If you look carefully enough, you will see lessons in almost everything your children do, and all you need to do is log them in the appropriate places.

If you are required to keep records for state regulations, be sure to follow their exact outline of what they expect and nothing more. Extra information will only complicate issues and open the door for potential interference. A number of companies offered packaged record keeping systems and computer programs that can make it easier for you also.

A last note—don't let the prospect of having to keep records be so daunting that is discourages you from homeschooling in the first place. As Larry and Susan Kaseman wrote in their book, *Taking Charge through Homeschooling: Personal and Political Empowerment,* "Valuable as records may be, they need to be kept in perspective. It does not make sense to spend so much time keeping records that there is not enough time for activities a family wants to do. Also, homeschooling should not be abandoned just because record keeping does not work well; another can be tried."

How do I homeschool children of different ages and levels?

With a lot of love and patience! Homeschooling children of multiple interests, ages and levels can be challenging, but also wonderful. Depending on the age of your kids, you can often cover the same topic for all of them in different ways. For instance, a lesson on how magnetism works might mean reading an essay on it for your older child, while your younger child goes around the house checking to see what things a magnet sticks to and what is doesn't, while your toddler is in the kitchen taking magnetic letters off the refrigerator and creating new art.

Older children sometimes find themselves helping younger ones and younger ones find themselves trying to imitate their elder siblings. Connections are made between your children that can be profound and lifelong. Of course, there are also days where all your children do is bicker and squabble, which is also quite natural. Those are the days when you will need to schedule some one on one time with each child in order to keep peace in the household. That time may be hard to find sometimes but Mary Griffith reassures everyone when she writes, "If you worry you won't be able to give each child enough time and attention, keep the problem in perspective: even if you can't give each of your children all the time they want with you, they're undoubtedly getting far more individual attention than they'd get in a school classroom."

What role do television and the Internet play in homeschooling?

Television seems to be both a blessing and a curse sometimes. On the positive side, it can introduce new and exciting ideas to your children, take them on journeys to faraway lands, show them interesting concepts, present different perspectives. On the negative side, it can numb their brains, teach them unwanted lessons, be used too often as a convenient babysitter and turn them into couch potatoes. Studies have shown that most homeschooling children spend far less time watching television overall than their public school counterparts, despite the fact that they are in the house more hours per day. Many homeschooling parents limit the time in front of the TV, and more than a few of them do not even own a TV set. How you choose to use your TV is up to you entirely; however, here are few helpful ideas:

- Don't use it as a reward or a punishment; it gives the television too much importance
- Consider putting the television in a little used room; children are less apt to ask for it if they don't see it
- Practice what you preach; don't watch an excessive amount of TV yourself and then tell the children they aren't allowed
- Record the shows you and the kids like the best and save them for days when a field trip is cancelled, the weather is bad, etc.
- Make television watching a family affair; watch the shows with your kids and discuss what you see
- Limit what shows your kids can see to the ones you know and

approve of; consider using it only for public television and other educational shows that tie in what you are studying

Another common question is whether you need a computer and access to the Internet to homeschool your children. Six years ago, I wrote that the Internet was a great tool but had little to do with success. Today, I have changed my thoughts on that somewhat. While *not* having a computer and/or net access should never be reason enough to not homeschool, I do feel that it is becoming a more essential tool everyday. So much research is done on the net today, and it offers so many online classes and learning possibilities. I would consider a good computer and net access to be very highly recommended.

Homeschooling families can use the net very effectively; it has great lessons, virtual field trips and scads of long distance learning for the educational department plus fun, friends and games. It opens the door to correspondence courses, online college classes and much more.

How can I help my kids stay safe while on the Internet?

A word of caution: as wonderful as the Internet is, it is just as dangerous, especially for young people. Precautions are quite necessary. Here are a few steps to keep in mind:
- warn your children of potential dangers of the net
- install a filtering or blocking program on your computer
- keep the computer out in the open where you can see what is being accessed
- don't allow personal information to be given out
- don't let your kids go into chat rooms without asking first

How do I teach a subject I dislike or don't understand myself?

There are several different options in this case. First of all, ask yourself if this is something your children really have to know and have to learn about right now. Just because you learned this particular subject matter in seventh grade doesn't mean your kids need to. Maybe you can wait until they develop their own interest in it and when that happens, you won't have to teach so much as guide them to good resources and information.

Second, you can choose to learn the subject right along with your children. Now that you are older and not being forced to learn it and then be graded on it, you may be pleasantly surprised to find that you like the subject after all. Learning material together can also strengthen the bond between you and your children, especially if they actually learn it faster than you do and you switch roles for a while—a real possibility with homeschooling.

Third, you can seek outside help with the subject. Can your spouse cover this one? How about a friend, neighbor or relative? You might hire a tutor for just this course or find a local mentor that can help you out. Find outside materials from the library or teacher's supply store and see if your children can teach them- selves this subject. They may find that they love it as much as you don't.

Also remember that it's okay to show our children that you don't like a subject and are going to tackle it nonetheless or find someone more qualified to help you do so. It's like admitting that you honestly don't like cucumbers. It makes it easier for them to admit that they don't like beets; they see it's just part of being human.

How do I know if my child is learning what he/she is "supposed to"?

Start by asking yourself why you think your child is "supposed" to know anything. That may sound strange but think about it for a minute. While there is some information that a child will need to know to keep safe and function in this world, there is also a lot of information that isn't necessary. For instance, knowing your name, address and phone number is important; knowing the main export of Bolivia isn't (unless you're looking to move there and then you will find out). Knowing how to add, subtract, multiply and divide is pretty important—they are vital to writing checks, earning money, paying taxes, keeping a job and so on. But is geometry necessary? It may be fun, it may be interesting and you may indeed find yourself using it in some future job—but will everyone? No, so why does everyone have to learn it?

Homeschooling can often be difficult for some parents because its tenets and possibilities sometimes run in opposition to what seems "right" or what is "supposed to be." Questioning these things can feel wrong or be very upsetting, but when it comes to homeschooling, it is almost inevitable. By recognizing that perhaps public school isn't the best way to educate your child, you are opening up the door to asking a lot of other questions, and some of them can make you uncomfortable. If you can, push past the discomfort and look seriously at the question. What do your children really need to know? When do they need to know it? What are they "supposed" to be taught? Why?

Because parents do worry about whether their children are learning what they are supposed to, whatever that might mean to them, they may decide to have their children tested now and then. Some states even require it. While the drive to do this is understandable, it is equally important that you realize that these national standardized tests are, in no way, an accurate measure of how your children are doing. They simply show how he or she is doing at that moment, on that subject, compared to public schoolers who may be (and most likely are) covering the material completely differently. The results can be interesting, but they aren't reliable, and taking tests only helps to perpetuate the concept that standardized tests are accurate summaries of how your child is doing. One mother whose six-year-old was tested recalls her response to the results. "They didn't know how to score her," she says. "She couldn't tell you the days of the week ("Daddy-goes-to-work days and Daddy-stays-home days") or the names of the months ("Spring, Fall, Winter and Christmas") but she had off-the-chart response to real life questions like what would you do if your house was on fire or if you found a wallet on the floor of a big store. The tester was especially confused," continued the mother, "when my daughter would finish her answer and then ask the tester what she would do in the same situation."

More importantly, these tests are not able to measure some of the most important things you will be teaching your children, things like compassion, responsibility, love and curiosity. How do these measure up next to knowing how to name the months of the year?

Take time ask yourself too—what is your personal underlying reason for wanting to test your children? Is it to evaluate how they are doing? It won't be accurate. It is because it is what you did when you were in school? Is it to prove to others that your child is learning and intelligent? There are much better and more effective and meaningful ways. Is it to find the areas where they are strongest and weakest? It won't likely let you know, however, it might give you some information on how well they can take a test. Is it to help prepare them for the future when they might have to take tests? That has validity, but it doesn't merit giving them more than a couple of tests and some basic instruction. There are too many test prep web sites and books available that you can use that are far preferable to actually putting your child through a test.

Instead, decide if your children are learning by observing them. Are they asking questions? Are they keeping busy? Are they happy? Have they learned things they didn't know before? Have they improved in something or some area? Examine the projects they have done, the awards and certificates they have earned, the journals or logs they have kept. Do you see progress and development there?

Don't expect them to be learning every single minute either; learning is sporadic. They may go through a period of soaking things up like a sponge and then seem to be doing nothing. That "nothing" time is when their brains are processing what they have learned. Think of the child learning to ride a bike. He takes several trips up and down the sidewalk with Dad or Mom hanging on for dear life, then he doesn't touch the bike for days. Suddenly, the next time out, before you can grab the shirt, he is off! Speeding down the sidewalk, hair blowing in the wind and screaming in delight (or is that you?). Those days of nothing were the ones where the brain laid down the pathways to know how to ride that bike. He is using the information that he has learned, and there are few better measures of success than that!

When asked the question of how a parent can measure how their children are doing in relation to their peers, Mary McCarthy, writer and homeschooling mom wrote, "Why would you want to? Your child is an individual. Celebrate the individual. No one is good at everything. No one is going to be perfect in every subject, so why would you want to compare your child to someone else's? Diversity is the blessing of humanity; individually, we lack in certain skills, but put together, we make a whole. If your child is learning—and enjoying it—that's success." The Lepperts agree when they wrote, "Homeschooling affords the student the opportunity to soar ahead in favored topics of study while spending more time on less popular academic areas. Keep in mind, grades are used in school settings mainly to keep children at one place and move others along."

How do I keep my children and myself motivated?

In other words, how do I prevent homeschool burnout? The best way to do this is to identify why it is happening in the first place and then fix that element. Just like the old saying advises you to not throw out the baby with the bath water, don't throw out homeschooling altogether because one aspect of it isn't working for you.

Burnout, no matter where it occurs, is due to stress; find the source of your stress and see what can be done about it. The number one reason for burnout in homeschooling is trying to do too much. This can come from several different directions. Perhaps you are trying to do too much within your homeschooling. Burnout is definitely higher in families that are trying to school at home in a very structured manner. It can be exhausting for parents and for kids, as each one of them struggles to meet standards and requirements they simply may not be up to—and don't need to be either. Lillian Jones, homeschooling mother and advocate, wrote, "The best homeschooling experience comes with no attempt to re-create school at home, and re-creating school at home is the single most stressful force against successful homeschooling. This message is hard to grasp sometimes, but it is a vital one. Pay heed."

Consider relaxing your approach to homeschooling so that scheduling and routine aren't as strict and inflexible. If you're in the middle of a unit on frogs, for example, and you're on the way to the bookstore to find a book on them, be willing to stop and watch a telephone pole going up, talk to a friend you haven't seen for a while or stop by the library and see what they have to offer. Interrupt your typical lessons with a field trip or by visiting an area expert on your topic and asking questions.

A majority of the parents who seem to experience burnout are also people who place great value in the ability to control things in life. In homeschooling, this can lead to trouble; give deep thought as to whether you really need to exert so much control here, or if you can relax and let go a little more. Give your children the opportunity to learn some self-control and influence the direction of their own educations; lighten up on some of your expectations and requirements and see where it leads you.

The pressure you are feeling may also be coming from trying to homeschool your kids and still do everything you did before. If you try to do all the cooking, cleaning, running errands and all the many other responsibilities of being an adult in the household, you will wear out quickly. This is the time to get help where you can. Have your partner either help with housework or take over some of the homeschooling. Make chores part of your children's daily curriculum. Hire a friend to come in and clean for you on a regular basis. Don't try to take on too much or it can all come crumbling down, and you will be miserable.

If you start feeling burnout creeping into the homeschooling picture, talk it out. Talk to your partner about it. Get his or her feedback and thoughts. Talk to your kids; where do you think the problem is stemming from? Their insights can be incredible. Talk to a friend, a neighbor, a relative. Pick someone who is supportive of homeschooling, however, or else you are apt to get the unwanted advice of "just put them in school!" Talk to others in your support group and complain a little; they have all been there, and they can often either just empathize so you don't feel so alone, or give you some useful ideas to try to help. If you can't see them in person, call or email them.

Sometimes you are feeling stressed out simply because you are generically stressed. Look at the rest of your life; are you sleeping well and long enough each night? How is your diet? Are you eating nutritious foods and enough of them? Are you getting any regular type of exercise? Have you had any time for just you lately? Time to read, relax, watch a movie, chat with a friend? If not, do so. You need that time to rejuvenate and refresh. Go to your favorite coffee shop alone. Meet a friend and go thrift store shopping. Take a walk through the park. Even doing errands alone can help. Remember, you certainly cannot homeschool well if you aren't taking care of the basics.

If all else fails, sit down and read your local newspaper or watch the news. Usually there is at least one horror story featured that will make you shake your head, feel pretty terrible for some kid and his parents, and make you bless the decision you've made for your own family.

Life isn't always smooth and easy; there are bad days whether you homeschool or not. When those lousy days happen, have back-up plans. Toss out the schoolwork and go to the library, the zoo, the museum, a friend's house, anywhere that is fun for all. Spend the day reading and coloring and building and dreaming. Enjoy your kids, their sense of humor, their joy in discovery, their unique perspectives on life. Have faith in yourself, in your children and in homeschooling, and that will carry you through to the next day when you make a completely new start.

"Stop thinking schoolishly. Stop acting teacherishly. Stop talking about learning as though it's separate from life." ~ Sandra Dodd, on how to do a quick installation of unschooling

In the Trenches

Homeschooling All Ages ~ Patti Kurdi

In my opinion, there are no right or wrong ways to homeschool multiple age groups; every family finds what works well for them. It has taken some time, but this is how I have finally coped with it.

My first goal is to get my children to develop a love of learning. I do this by example; I show how I can learn also from all the materials being taught. Secondly, once they are readers, I teach them to develop independent learning styles. I think that is especially important for children who want to continue their education. Colleges have been known to recruit homeschoolers because they believe they have stronger independent learning abilities.

The following is what a typical day is like in my home. My twelfth grader has come to the conclusion that she needs more than one teacher, so we decided to incorporate Internet homeschooling. We have all courses available to us, including teachers and counselors to assist as needed. She gets up in the morning just as though she is about to attend outside school. She checks in at 7 a.m. and independently studies the necessary subjects. If need be, she contacts the teachers for online conferences. I do all the grading and testing, and I work hand-in-hand with her Web teachers to assist my daughter in gaining as much as possible from the course work.

My third grader is a different story. Each week, I prepare the necessary coursework for the upcoming week. We begin the day with a mile run, breakfast, clean up, and then the books. Because he can read on his own, he goes over his instructions and then follows through on them. This is probably one of my most successful teachings. You can teach a child the basics like reading and counting, but if you can teach him to be an independent learner, you've accomplished something wonderful. I am always there to answer questions, give tests, and assist him in his experiments.

Then there are my preschoolers. I run a small business and have preschool hour twice a day. On one hand, it is the hardest age to teach, but on the other, it is the most exciting. We use arts and crafts to teach almost everything. My third grader loves to take breaks from his work and assist in teaching the other kids. Sometimes, the craft requires more than one adult, and this is where my own children help me out. The preschoolers look up to my kids like they were their own brother and sister. They are fine role models for the younger students.

We do more than coursework. We attend Park Day twice a week for three hours with children ranging from eight months to 16 years old. Twice a month we go to Kid's Club for workshops, and we love incorporating field trips to zoos, museums, plays, farms, beaches, and local companies who are willing to teach our children about our community.

When teaching several age groups, I have used separate course work for each grade, but still try to bring the children together as much as possible. This has helped to develop a love for learning, and it has reinforced my children's love and respect for each other. This not something taught in your local public or private school. I allow for age appropriate course work, but always find a way to integrate the different ages together. After all, the world is full of different ages, colors, and beliefs. This is just a part of learning to be together and have mutual respect regardless of those differences.

In the Trenches

Homeschooling on Wheels ~ Peg Wood

In the spring of 2004, my husband and I had finally come to a decision to pull our two girls out of public school and to begin a life of homeschooling. The decision was years in the making, but we felt it was time to take back control of their education. Since it was spring, we decided to let the girls finish out the school year and begin homeschooling in the fall.

On the heels of this life change, my husband came home and informed me that there was a possible job change as well. An MRI colleague had mentioned that there are human resource companies that provide medical personnel to hospitals and clinics across the country on a temporary or permanent basis; this is called *locum tenens* or "stand in." Could we travel as a family across the United States working at hospitals or clinics in need for 13 -15 weeks at a time? We have always traveled (I was born and married into the military) and after trying to settle down for the last three years, it seemed as though gold had literally been dropped into our laps!

Our first step was to read a few books on homeschooling. Nothing sticks out in my mind as far as which book helped us the most but all were very valuable in guiding us in our homeschooling choice. We amassed a large number of books to use as references since we had decided to go with an eclectic style of schooling rather than buy curriculum. Some books we had already been using as references at home, but we could always use more! We even bought a telescope, electronic globe and microscope set to get us started. I filed the necessary papers with the state and informed the school district that our girls would be homeschooled starting in the fall. I also got copies of all their medical and shot records. The HR company would provide us with a furnished apartment so it was fairly easy to pack what we needed into our conversion van. The only problem we ever ran into was packing what we *wanted* along with what we *needed*; space was a premium. But we narrowed it down to a tote for each of our girls' personal belongings, three bookshelves full of school supplies, three sets of drawers made of plastic for clothes and a few odd and ends to fill out the nooks and crannies. We emptied the house of most everything and condensed our material possessions into an 8 x 10' storage area. Our thought was that we would travel for two years to get a feel for it, and if we didn't like it we could always go back home.

Our first job assignment coincided with the beginning of the school year. At first we were literally re-creating school in the home. The girls found it boring, frustrating and limiting. After all, wasn't homeschooling supposed to include a student-led element? We kept a pretty rigorous routine for the first month, and then it all fell to pieces. We weren't as organized as we should have been considering we were putting the curriculum together ourselves. So, we decided to just enjoy the area and take advantage of opportunities as they presented themselves. In other words, we decided to unschool. It felt weird not using all of the books we had bought, but we were all happier with the life learning. There were so many things to do that we had to pick and choose which activities we would accomplish before our job assignment was over. It worked out very well. The local homeschool group was always doing some fun field trip or meeting for the weekly rock climbing session, so we were always engaged, and I could see the girls were very happy with the change. We would crack open a book or two on occasion but for the most part; we simply enjoyed each others' company and the dailiness of life.

Our second location wasn't as successful. We did find a local homeschool group and plenty of opportunities to be socially engaged, but it lacked an element we had come to really appreciate: the field trip! The homeschool group was geared to meeting the social needs of the children and felt that if a family wanted to go on a field trip, then they would plan one and invite the rest to come along. Since we were only in the area for three months, finding, researching and planning for a field trip became a true impossibility. So we decided to take advantage of the situation and enjoy the social group we had come to appreciate. However, we did get the girls involved in music lessons. Our oldest daughter took to it like a duck to water. Our youngest did enjoy her music lessons but wasn't as single-minded about it as her sister. Toward the end of the three month assignment, we re-evaluated what we were packing in our van. We had three bookcases full of school supplies and were using only a fraction of them. So, we decided to stick with good reference books, like atlases, dictionaries, thesauruses, etc. and to put aside the special interest or single topic books and workbooks. We sent them back to our house to be stored with the rest of our belongings.

By the third job assignment we were starting to get the idea of letting go of expectations for what we would find at each location. We had been fortunate to find great social groups in our first two assignments, but our third job started at the beginning of summer. We didn't know that most homeschool groups take a break like the rest of the public school system. So, while we had wonderful opportunities to enjoy local activities, we weren't as social as we wanted to be. By the end of the summer my husband and I started to panic that our girls weren't getting what they needed academically. We still had the public school mind set so we decided to buy a curriculum. All went well for the first two months but then we moved to our fourth job location and it disrupted the well oiled machine we had created.

We hit the jackpot on our fourth job assignment. It was a large metropolitan city that offered everything socially, educationally, and geographically. Our homeschooling became piecemeal again, but we made up for it with art classes, music lessons, cultural events and a strong local homeschool group. We ended up staying a full year for that job assignment. It was hard to say good-bye but traveling has taught us we never really have to say "good-bye." Our job can take us back to the places we've loved, and with technological gadgets it's very easy to remain in contact with friends we've made.

We are beginning our fourth year of homeschooling/traveling, and the routine for setting up in a new place is pretty well set: find the local library and get a card, Google any area homeschool groups, find a new church, find any and all museums or zoos and see if there are any classes offered to homeschool families. We have since abandoned the apartment choice and live full-time in an RV. We have to be judicious with our choices of what to pack because of the weight limit, but it's not as bare bones as it was in the beginning. We are still using a curriculum but we have settled into a Monday – Friday schedule with only two subjects a day, so we have plenty of time to enjoy the local faire. I think it's the best of traditional homeschooling and unschooling. We have a few workbooks to supplement the material but if we find we need an extra book or two we get it from the library. The challenge comes when my girls take an interest in a particular thing—perhaps a science class—and the area doesn't provide what we need. But as I said earlier, we've learned to take advantage of opportunities as they come. Each place offers something special or unique we couldn't have done if we stayed close to home. And if the girls were truly insistent about a particular class or subject, there are plenty of useful websites where we could either work online or purchase the materials to use at home. I have a few websites saved under "My Favorites," but I use them pretty infrequently; only when I think it will add a little more to what we're learning about at the time.

And while it may seem to some that it is unfair to drag our children from place to place without giving them the opportunity to set down roots, let me reassure you that my girls wouldn't have it any other way. We've often spoken about the challenges and delights that come with traveling every 3-6 months: making friends and then leaving, being in some places better suited to us than others, seeing so much of the country, enjoying local events. My children understand the difficulties and work to overcome them because they feel those difficulties are far outweighed by the opportunities and wonderful experiences they wouldn't otherwise have. I am often approached by adults we've met in the community, and they tell me how surprised they are with my girls' outgoing natures. The comment is usually, "They seem like they've been here forever!"

The Voices of Experience

Unschooling Adventures ~ Nancy and Bill Greer

The decision to homeschool is very personal. Our culture makes it easy to send children to school, so parents must have a strong motivation to defy the norm and keep their children at home. While I can't tell you why every parent decides to homeschool, I can tell you about our family and how we became unschoolers.

Nancy is a person who likes to plan ahead. Before our first child was born, she started making plans for their education. We discussed the pros and cons of public schools versus private schools. Nancy lived practically all her life in the same house in Northern Virginia and attended public school where she was subjected to an "experimental-program-of-the-month" education during the 1960s and 1970s. She remembers starting school as an outgoing child who enjoyed reading to her classmates, but somewhere along the way becoming shyer and developing a fear of speaking in public. She did well academically, but just didn't enjoy going to school. Some of her strongest memories include the year that "mainstreaming" put older kids with developmental and behavioral problems in her class, and one boy held her by the wrists over a stairwell and threatened to drop her. She also remembers the morning she felt sick and wanted to leave, but by the time the teacher finally acknowledged her raised hand and called her to the front of the room, it was too late and she threw up on the teacher's desk.

I grew up as a Navy brat and attended about a dozen different schools. Like Nancy, I also did well academically, but unlike her, I viewed my public school experience fairly positively, and wasn't as inclined to opt for private school for our children. Besides, I figured we were going to be such supportive parents that the actual school environment wasn't very important. Our involvement could make up for any of the shortcomings of the school.

We started out evaluating and visiting lots of private schools and public schools. As we checked out the public schools, we found they weren't the same as when we attended. Classes were larger, students did more poorly, and weapons and drugs were much more commonplace. My frugal (okay, cheap) nature rebelled against the idea of stretching our finances to pay thousands of dollars for a private school, but I was beginning to think it might be our only option, and so we visited several private schools. We liked many of the philosophies and approaches we came across, but we ended up feeling that there were major shortcomings at each school. For us, the perfect program would involve combining the best ideas from two or three different schools. We also realized that most private schools were based on the same model of the public schools, only "more" and "better." They had more computers, more hands-on activities, better student/teacher ratios, better discipline, etc. We slowly came to realize that we didn't just want a better version of public school education; we wanted something completely different.

We had heard about homeschooling from various sources and decided we wanted to read more about it. We checked out a handful of books from the public library, including ones written by John Holt and the Colfax family. In defending sending our kids to public school, I had argued that parental involvement was more important than the actual school they went to. How could you have more parental involvement than homeschooling? With the private schools, we had wished for one that combined the best of the different philosophies and techniques we saw at the various schools we visited. With homeschooling, we could pick and choose the best methods for our family. We were even more convinced when a careful self-evaluation made us realize that our important life skills, the activities we enjoyed doing for fun or as hobbies, and the most of our job skills had all been learned outside of school! By the time our firstborn was a year old, we had decided to continue educating him at home.

During those early years of childrearing, we got to experience the wonders of learning new things through the eyes of a child. We saw how children are the ultimate scientists, exploring and experimenting with everything. They learn by trial and error and are able to master difficult tasks such as walking and talking with virtually no instruction. Despite these observations, I still wasn't likely to be a natural unschooler. I tend to be a "here, let me show you had to do that" type of person. Fortunately, our son Glen was able to teach me to be an unschooler pretty quickly. He wanted to do things himself, and if I tried to help him, he got mad! I discovered that whenever I offered unasked-for help, it was almost guaranteed that Glen would not only ignore my offered advice, he would stop trying completely.

Nancy likes to research anything she gets involved with and was more widely read than I was when it came to homeschooling. She directed me to some good books and articles that soon made me an unschooling convert. I love to tinker and experiment to figure things out for myself and often disliked it when someone would take away that pleasure of learning by telling me what to do without checking to see if I wanted any help. Unschooling started to really make sense to me! Someone once told me that in a conversation with John Holt, Ivan Illich compared education to eating an orange. I can imagine him describing the whole process—the feel of the orange against your fingers as you peel it, the sharp citric smell and the sticky juice that might squirt when you bite into a section of the orange, the seeds you have to spit out. The modern education establishment would declare such a process too messy and inefficient. It would be distilled to a few essentials with the result that a vitamin C tablet would be considered a superior substitute. How could anyone compare the sensual pleasure of eating an orange to swallowing a vitamin tablet?

With the fervor of any new convert, we were eager to share our ideas and to discuss unschooling with others. We decided to start the Family Unschoolers Network and use a newsletter to help unschoolers support each other. That was the start of FUN News. We also were involved with starting a local support group. With her love for researching her interests, Nancy began to build an extensive collection of resources. She carted a file box of articles, newspaper clippings, and books to our meetings. She wrote a resource column in FUN News to share much of the information she came across.

Many of the books we liked were not easily available. To satisfy our own voracious appetite for new books and to help the many homeschoolers who asked us where they could find the resources recommended, Nancy decided we should start a bookstore. FUN Books was born with a handful of titles and a handful of customers. From the beginning, it was important to us to show homeschoolers that there was an alternative to pre-packaged curriculum materials and that learning really can be a fun process for the whole family.

Over the years, we have seen that new homeschoolers have a tendency to want to start off with a prepared curriculum, but the longer they continue, the more they are likely to relax and feel comfortable choosing individual materials to use in a personalized program. Unschooling becomes an even more important learning approach as our world is becoming a place of more rapid changes.

For unschoolers, learning is a continuous process and that makes them more adaptable to change. When learning comes from a sense of purpose and a high degree of self-motivation, it is more likely to be an enjoyable process that is embraced rather than a process that is viewed as drudgery to be avoided if possible. Learning how to learn is perhaps the most important lesson of unschooling, and keeping the experience enjoyable and rewarding helps ensure that unschoolers can learn what they need to know when they need to know it. It's just-in-time-learning for our fast changing world.

As homeschooling grows and becomes more mainstream, there are more people who recognize that an advantage of homeschooling is the freedom to throw out traditional educational approaches and to try alternative approaches that can work better for your family. Unfortunately, there are also more companies marketing to homeschoolers and promoting the idea that homeschooling means bringing the school process home or that homeschooling is just a less expensive private school. They are happy to sell you curriculum materials or sign you up for their programs. These companies have their place, but it is important that they not drown out the voices of the alternatives. If homeschooling becomes too regulated and too standardized, it runs the risk of becoming just another form of public education and will lose many of its benefits. If we're lucky, the opposite will happen and public education will become more like unschooling!

The Greers founded Family Unschoolers Network and formerly published FUN News. You can find them online at www.unschooling.org or write to them at 1688 Bellhaven Woods Court., Pasadena, MD 21122-3727

Chapter 4

Where Can I Find Help?

"Much education today is monumentally ineffective. All too often we are giving young people cut flowers when we should be teaching them to grow their own plants."

~ John W. Gardner
president of the Carnegie Corporation

How do I find a local support group?

Finding a local support group is usually not a difficult process, depending on how large the city is that you are living in. Check your local newspaper for announcements of group meetings and calendars. If you run into other homeschoolers, ask them for assistance. Check out the bulletin boards at libraries, bookstores, children's stores and churches. Many of the homeschooling magazines list state-by-state contacts as well, so find a recent issue and see what is listed under your state. If you have access to the web, check there for state web sites or go to national web sites and see if they list regional representatives. These support groups will be your key to keeping up to date about homeschooling activities/events/conferences, legislation and current court cases. They are key to your networking with others in all realms of home-schooling from the next door neighbor to your Congressman.

How do I find a state support group?

Your best sources are homeschooling books, magazines, local support groups, the Internet, and perhaps your state Department of Education if you have made the choice to be in contact with them. Sometimes schools will have this information also.

How do I find a national support group?

Once again, look in homeschooling books and magazines and on the Internet. Often in searching for one of these groups, you are going to run into information about the others also. Before joining one, check out what is available so that you can compare. Pay close attention to the group's mission statement for their organization to make sure it is in line with your homeschooling beliefs and foundations.

How do I start my own support group?

Sometimes the group in your area isn't meeting your needs or perhaps is too far away to get to on a regular basis. In this case, you might want to start your own. Here are some guidelines on how to do it:

I. Set your mission or goal

In other words, what are you looking for in this group? List what you hope to achieve and ask the following questions of both yourself and anyone else who is interested in forming this new group.

A. Will this group bye a casual, informal group or more structured?

Is everyone going to be friends and socialize together, meeting for coffee and play dates or will this group be primarily for setting up field trips and events?

B. Will the group be religious-based, secular or a mixture?

Some groups require members to sign a "statement of faith" to belong. Is this something that you want to do? Do you want to make it optional or mandatory? Do you want to welcome all faiths to your group? What about Muslims, Hindus, atheists, and others?

C. How large should the group be?

The larger a group is, the more structure will be needed. All sizes have their benefits: large groups can organize better events while smaller ones get to know each other better. Do you want to set a limit? Before you answer that, think about where you will meet (how big is it?), what you will do (will there be food? activities?), and how you will or will not keep track of members (will you have a newsletter, phone tree, email directory?)

D. Where should the group meet?

Most groups start out in churches, community centers or members' homes. This can work well or it can become a nightmare if the group is too successful and grows too large. Libraries and other public buildings often have meeting rooms available at no charge, so check around your area and make a list of possibilities.

E. How often should the group meet?

It typically varies from once a week to once a month. What day and time is best?

F. Do you want officers? Dues?

While there are perks to this, it also makes things more complicated and requires more time.

G. Do you want children to come to the meetings?

If so, remember the facility will have to be big enough to accommodate everyone. If not, many families will not come because part of their homeschooling philosophy is to keep parents and kids together.

H. What will you name the group?

The name, if you have one, will probably be used in promotion and in contacting other families and community groups. Give it some thought. Many people create some kind of acronym for their group that is easy to use and remember.

I. Look at other homeschooling groups in your area.

See what you do and do not like about the groups. Use that information in forming your own group.

II. Promote your group

The primary ways to get word out about your new group are:

A. Regular announcements

Place them in newspapers, including what you did at the last meeting and the agenda for the next one. Make these sound exciting and always include an invitation for other families to come and check out the group.

B. Advertise on television or radio

If your local cable company has a channel for local advertising, ask if your non- profit group can advertise for no charge. Put public service announcements on radio stations in your area.

C. List your group on local, safe internet sites

Have information about your group on local sites that list community events and other activities.

D. Create your group web site

Have one of your computer-savvy moms/dads/kids create a web site for your group. List meeting times, location and other information.

E. Create flyers

Hand them out at church, the library, teacher supply stores, etc.

F. Names and numbers

Leave your name and number at the most common places people ask for homeschooling information. If you are called, invite the caller to the next meeting. Take his or her name and address for your files and send them notices of upcoming meetings or events.

G. Hold open houses

Host this event regularly for new families to come and ask their questions and have the chance to meet other homeschoolers.

H. Speaking engagements

Offer to speak about homeschooling at your local library or other public places. Hand out flyers and other information.

I. Talk to everyone you can

Word of mouth is always the best type of advertising. If you hear someone asking about homeschooling, speak up. Talk to the family in the library.

III. Maintain your group

To keep growing strong, be sure to:

A. Organize a telephone or email chain

This way each member is responsible to contact the next to remind him or her of upcoming meetings and events. You can also set up some kind of special interest group on sites like Google and Yahoo. These allow members to email the entire group or each other with questions, problems, encouragement and advice.

B. Plan a number of different activities

This will help to make sure you are meeting the needs of all the families in your group. For example, if you only have children under the age of six, it's easy to only think of activities for that age. However, you need to offer events for adolescents and teens as well.

C. Check with other members often

See if there are improvements, changes or problems that need to be discussed. Give them a chance to give you feedback at all times.

Lastly, be patient. Creating a support group that is strong and growing is a gradual process and not likely to happen overnight. It can take some groups a year to feel they are on track and getting what they need. It is definitely worth the work, however, to have a place you can go to and people you can be with that make you feel welcome and comfortable.

What kind of field trips are available?

This is a little like asking where can I go for vacation? The possibilities are virtually endless; the only boundaries are your time, money and imagination.

Many homeschooling groups will have field trips set up for a month or more at a time and you can participate in them. However, many times the field trips your children will like the best are the one you personally set up for them. If you keep your eyes open at all times, you will be astonished at all the places and people there are out there who would make terrific field trips for your family. Here are just a few of the places you can choose from:

- rivers/mountains/caves/forests—whatever your area has to offer
- doctors/hospitals/medical centers

- factories
- theatres
- restaurants
- churches
- museums
- colleges
- stores
- government buildings
- libraries
- historic sites
- YMCA/YWCA
- experts and their businesses

Once you have targeted a place to go, contact the place and ask to talk to the person who is responsible for setting up field trips. Arrange the day and time that is convenient, and be sure to ask how many children can comfortably come, what ages are welcome, and if you should bring money for any reason. Get any directions you might need and prepare your list of questions before you go, so you are prepared.

You can follow up your field trips with various crafts to make, books to read and discussions to have. Don't focus too hard on making the field trip a lesson, however. Instead, make it a fun time where children also happen to learn things, albeit not always the things you think they are going to learn. One mother, for example, was on the way to a museum field trip in an area she was not familiar with, and soon she was lost. Instead of giving up and going home, however, she stopped at a nearby bagel shop for a snack, and her three children ended up following the business complex's window washer around finding out all about his work.

Virtual field trips, taken over the Internet, can be fun for your kids too. They aren't as wonderful as the real thing, but on days when money is short, the weather is rotten or the energy is in short supply, they are a nice alternative.

Why should I go to a homeschool conference?

My first reaction to this question is why *wouldn't* you go to a homeschool conference, but that is because I am biased. When I first started homeschooling, I found these conferences to be like blood transfusions. They reenergized everything from head to toe. In the first book, I compared them to that first cup of coffee in the morning (even though I don't drink coffee) because conferences wake you up, rev you up and get you going with more energy and enthusiasm than you had before (and without the caffeine!).

There are two main reasons that you will want to attend a homeschooling conference: to take the classes and to network with the other people you meet. The classes offered often supply the answers to your questions and provide information you can take home and apply immediately (or even on the way home in the car!). Just as importantly, however, these conferences allow you to be immersed in and surrounded by people who think a lot like you do—they share the same worries and wonders, dilemmas and delights. Just sitting around talking with all of them can be enough to send you home brimming with confidence. One mother, after attending her first conference was heard to exclaim, "This is better than Christmas! I've never felt so comfortable and accepted anywhere else in my life!"

An additional perk to these gatherings are the vendors that line the hallways. All of them have a service or product to offer homeschoolers and they are great fun to look at, ponder and sometimes purchase. You might find just the book you needed for your history unit, a complete curriculum that fits one of your children or just a nifty toy for your preschooler to play with on the trip home. Many conferences also have a bookstore set up. The materials here are frequently enough to make the trip worthwhile. If you're on a strict budget, make sure you stick to your list. The temptation to buy one of everything is often overwhelming.

Homeschooling conferences are often held on different levels, depending on who is sponsoring them. If you live in a sizable city, there may be some offered locally. Most states have their own conferences and some groups hold an annual conference for families from across the country. They can be found on different homeschooling websites and magazines and are frequently listed in local homeschooling newsletters and announcements.

Before you pay your money and pack your bags, however, request a conference brochure which will tell you all the details of the event, such as keynote speakers, children's activities, accommodation costs, food arrangements and so on. Once you have the brochure, look through it carefully so you can mark which classes and speakers you want to see the most, as well as what classes your spouse or children might want to attend.

Also make sure that the theme or philosophy of the conference either meshes with yours or at least is intriguing enough that you want to know more about it. It is okay to go to a conference that emphasizes structured homeschooling if you are unschooling or a religious conference if you are of another or no faith, but you should know that beforehand, so you can make that decision rather than be surprised.

Check to see what the conference's policies are regarding children. Some welcome them and even offer special programming for them, while others prefer you do not bring any children other than nursing babies. (If this is the case, find out why. This is not the typical attitude found in homeschooling events.) If children aren't welcome in classes, you will need to make some alternative childcare arrangements. Older children can be left at home, but younger children cannot unless dad or grandparents are going to be present. Consider bringing a homeschooled teen, parent, partner or friend with you to entertain the kids while you attend the conference.

Whether you are a novice or a veteran, a good homeschooling conference can be a real blessing. Try to find a space in your budget to fit in at least once a year. The actual expenses typically break down to:

- the cost of the conference (per person or family rates)
- the cost of getting to and from the conference (gas, etc.)
- the cost of eating while you are at the conference (bring your own, eat in the room, or eat with the others attendees)
- the cost of lodging (hotel, camping, sharing a room, etc.)
- the cost of potential child care (friend, teen, etc.)

Conferences can cost several hundred dollars but many families feel they are more than worth the expense. "We consider this a family vacation," said one mother of four. "We wouldn't miss it for anything."

How do I talk with school officials?

Carefully. Very, very carefully. There are some wonderful school officials out there who only want the best for your child, and they will support you in your decision to homeschool as much as possible. Unfortunately, this is not usually the case.

When you are in contact with school personnel, do as little talking as possible. Find out exactly what they want to know, as well as what they legally have a right to know and then provide only that information. Stop there. As much as you might want to share the miracle of your non-reader sitting up in bed until 2 a.m. reading, it is unlikely they will share your joy. Instead, you may find yourself labeled as negligent for clearly not caring enough about your child's well being to make sure he gets enough rest each night.

Will the State Department of Education help me?

If you ask most veteran homeschoolers this question, please don't be offended by the erupting laughter that ensues. It is a little like asking your OB if he could refer you to a good home birth midwife. Because of the conflict of interests, it is rare for one side to help the other.

The answer to the question is . . . very unlikely.

The vast majority of homeschoolers who do not have to contact their State Department of Education choose not to simply because they see no reason for it. They don't want their input or their interference. If you live in a state that requires registration and contact with your DOE, then either move or provide only what they legally can ask for and nothing else. If you don't have to be in contact with them, please don't. Too many times they will give you misinformation, telling you you need to turn in material or information that you do not actually have to, scaring you into thinking you are not capable of educating your own children and, as a number of families can attest, trying to convince you that you have bitten off far more than you can chew. While there are certainly DOEs that are informed, supportive and understanding, they are the exception to the rule.

What if there aren't any homeschoolers close to us?

If you live in an area that is remote and you have little access to local homeschoolers, you will have to depend largely on regional, state and national support groups and organizations for your advice, encouragement and assistance.

Make sure there really aren't any homeschoolers in your area. There may be some you aren't aware of simply because they have kept it quiet. Ask permission to post something in your church, library or grocery store, and list your phone number or email address so others can get in touch with you.

This is one situation when a computer in the house would be very helpful. There are chat rooms for homeschoolers of all ages and they can be wonderful outlets when you or your children need to rant, spout, brag or just be reminded there are a lot of others just like you out there.

In the Trenches

Why a Former School Teacher Chose to Homeschool
~ Francy Stillwell

This afternoon after lunch, I had the privilege of snuggling with my kids on the sofa and watching an old episode of "Perry Mason." I fully appreciate how lucky I am to get to do this with them. We almost led a different life until I decided one day that society had a warped idea of how we are supposed to live, and I didn't have to comply.

I worked as a public school teacher for 10 years. While I started out very idealistic and enthusiastic about it, over the years, I became increasingly disheartened about the whole public school system. It felt like my students came in the door hating school and me before I had even been given a chance. As hard as I tried to be "up" on the current information about learning, I found no support about applying that knowledge from my administrator or very many fellow teachers. Worse, some of the students were becoming alarmingly violent at younger and younger ages. Finally, during my seventh year, I realized just how incredibly dysfunctional the public school system was and that the way to change things was not from within. I was tired—tired of being constantly exposed to viruses and stress; tired of having to teach developmentally inappropriate, irrelevant content, tired of seeing violent kids being kept in school and jeopardizing everyone's safety just to keep their dropout rates low. I was weary of hearing the excuse, "This is/isn't what is best for kids," when I knew that what was good for one kid isn't necessarily good for another. It was a one-size-fits-all system, and if it failed to work, the child was viewed as the problem, not the system.

I came to see schools as a factory processing children as its main product—and not very successfully at that. Over the years, I watched as more and more students and teachers became angry, disaffected, burned out, broken, and violent. I am not ashamed to say I felt some of this, too.

Then, I had my own two children, one 21 months after the other.

It was killing me to have to drop my babies off at daycare each day. We had a wonderful daycare provider, but my children were spending the day with someone other than me, and it felt wrong. In my heart I knew they would not be children for long, and I wanted to be a part of as much of their lives as possible.

Four years ago, after surviving my tenth year as a public school teacher, I quit. Somehow, we made it work financially—just. There have been a few times when I have had my doubts about whether we're doing the right thing. My husband certainly had his doubts too, but time has shown us both some outstanding results. Our kids are filled with a growing creative spirit that isn't being squelched in the name of institutional socialization. On the contrary, I get to see their creative processes grow on a daily basis. They are getting firsthand experience at being valuable citizens in our society—they get to be kids. All life experiences create potential for learning, and we feel good that we are preparing them for life in this world, the way it really is—you know—LIFE, mixed with real people of all ages, shapes, colors, and cultures. LIFE—something to survive and thrive in. That just doesn't happen in schools.

There is always a concern from others that my children may not be "getting enough socialization." I guess these folks think I keep them locked up all day. Quite the contrary; we are out in the world on a daily basis. We take part in a variety of groups and classes. We go to museums and parks; we know our neighbors. In school, children are learning about the world from each other—equally inexperienced peers. The result is not acceptable.

People seem relieved that I am a teacher when they discover we are homeschooling, and I just have to laugh when they say this. To be honest, there isn't much about my teaching experience that is helpful except as a model of what not to do.

I now find joy in every day. I feel so grateful to have this time with our children. Both of them are curious, and we can pursue things while they are still feeling curious. I endeavor to expose them to all kinds of things so that they will have something new all the time. I try hard to listen to them so I can be an effective guide, and if I listen carefully enough, they are guides for me as well. And sometimes, we have lunch, snuggle on the sofa—and watch an old episode of "Perry Mason."

"I am always ready to learn but I do not always like being taught."
~ Winston Churchill, former Prime Minister of England

Voices of Experience

Dealing with the Rest of the World ~ Pat Montgomery

Pat Montgomery is the retired president and founder of Clonlara Home-Based Education in Ann Arbor, Michigan. You can find out more about their programs at www.clonlara.org

As founder and director of Clonlara School, I bring to this essay my experience in advocating for families who enroll in our home based education program. I have taught in public, parochial, and alternative schools for my entire career—all 47 years of it. The following is advice that we regularly prescribe. It can be applied to any home educating family, I believe.

The whole idea behind Clonlara School's philosophy is "do it yourself," seize the power, take control. But early on in the home education movement, it became abundantly clear to me that parents were on the low rung of the power structure when dealing with public school officials. Only students were lower on the ladder. In the late seventies/early eighties, most local school officials took grave issue with the notion of home education. Some scoffed; others threatened.

A father in Northern Ohio was arrested and jailed in 1980 for teaching his seven year old at home. Another Michigan was jailed for two weeks for home educating his eight youngsters. These are but two examples of the animosity that existed. Parents justifiably felt that there on the opposite side of the trenches in a war. They were, after all, denying the public schools coveted tax monies by removing or not sending their children to be counted on the school rolls.

It was clear to me that parents could not face this foe alone, so one of the first things Clonlara School established in its array of services was to become a team with parents. As a credentialed school official myself, I was able to interact with, and for, parents when they dealt with school authorities, prosecuting attorneys, judges, social services workers, social security authorities, college admissions officers, and others. The result of this unified approach was that outside officials were persuaded to deal in a respectful manner with parents.

Clonlara School filed suit in federal court against school superintendents, truant officers (a.k.a. pupil personnel directors), boards of education, and the Michigan Department of Education for denying the rights of parents to educate their own children. We lost that suit, but another that we filed simultaneously in Circuit Court in 1985, *Clonlara v. Michigan Board of Education,* was a major success. The Michigan Board of Education was ultimately restricted to treating home educating parents exactly the way it treated nonpublic schools.

So much for early history! Has the scene changed? Are today's public school officials dealing fairly with parents? Yes and no. More of them are, but far too many are not. These latter take a proprietary stand. They resent having nonprofessionals (parents) insert themselves into the sacrosanct arena of schooling. They deal with students similarly. It is not uncommon to hear of boards of education that forbid public school students to invite home educated students to a school dance, for example. When students transfer from home to their local public high school, it is not unusual for them to be threatened with denial of credits earned through home schooling.

So, what's a parent to do? How can they deal with hostile officials?

The most successful step they can take, in my albeit slightly biased opinion, is to enroll in Clonlara School. We attend to all of the administrative duties associated with their home education, chief among which is dealing with all contacts with officials. For over 20 years, I have witnessed the substantial difference that this makes in parents' and students' lives. Clonlara stands alone in providing this service. It makes a great deal of difference to school officials and to other outside officials when they learn that the family is willing to receive guidance and counseling from a school. Having school people dealing with other school people puts the issues on a different level entirely.

A parent does well to learn what the regulations are. Knowledge of the law on compulsory school attendance and on home education is essential, first off. Librarians have this information. State senators and representatives can supply it. Local home school support groups have it. It is spelled out clearly in the volumes of education law for each state. Knowing the regulations is a must. Knowing one's rights is the corollary.

Perhaps the most devastating thing that I have observed amongst parents is that they lack self-confidence when dealing with authorities. They are, in this sense, victims of an upbringing and/or schooling that renders them virtually powerless. These are capable people who can run a successful household, fix appliances, operate costly equipment, diagnose illnesses, and so on…yet they cower before the school principal. It puts them at a decided disadvantage. We are, after all, just humans. We deserve respect and dignity. We are equals. That fact seems to have gotten lost.

When contacted by school people, parents do well to act in a respectful, dignified way. They also do well to get everything in writing. It is far too easy, when talking informally to a principal, teacher, or school clerk, for example, to omit or to gloss over important pieces of information. School (and other officials) are themselves sticklers for getting things in writing; so ought parents to be. It is perfectly reasonable to respond to a telephone call by stating, "I don't want to discuss matters by phone; please put whatever it is you wish to tell me into writing; I will respond with more intelligence then." Spoken firmly and politely, that is a professional approach.

Clonlara recommends to its families when they are withdrawing children from public or private schools, for instance, to do it in writing. A courtesy note simply stating that the child "is no longer enrolled" in that public (or private) school can be slipped into a cumulative file folder. This assures a parent that the message was received and understood.

A telephone conversation is not as effective, and it leaves the parent open to all manner of prying. Acting with dignity invites the same treatment from the school officials.

Many parents assume that they must give lengthy explanations about what they intend to do, why they arrived at the decision, and the like. This is simply not so. A parent's decision is his own; he needs explain it to no one.

Relatives of a family that chooses to home educate are, sad to say, often the violators of parents' rights. Those who disagree with a parent's decision to home educate have been known to make anonymous reports to social services agencies accusing the parents of child abuse or neglect. Of course, social workers are not at liberty to divulge the name(s) of the complaining party, and they are responsible to check out the complaint.

Should this happen, parents must be aware, once again, of their rights. They are, for example, under no obligation to answer a knock or doorbell. Clonlara recommends that they do not. The social worker will leave a business card. The parent then has a chance to assess the situation and to respond *on his/her terms* rather than being caught unawares. Make the call; arrange an appointment—this can often be in the office of the social worker—at a time when both parents can be present or when a trusted friend and advocate can come along. The parent is cooperating and can better hear and understand and respond to the allegations.

One parent reported that she was doing kitchen work when two men, one a sheriff's deputy, rang the doorbell of her rural home. She ignored the ring and went about her business despite the fact that the men could see her through the window. After trying repeatedly to get her attention, the duo left. She retrieved the card stuck into the doorframe and phoned me. I had a call in to the social worker before he returned to his desk. He was irate that she didn't answer the doorbell. How dare she? Was she deaf? I asked him whether he would recommend that a young mother with two young children ought to automatically respond to the ring when two strange men were at the door—in a rural area like her own or in an urban one. He agreed that this could be dangerous and then he calmed down enough to address the reason for his visit rationally. The public school bus driver had reported that he saw children at the home but they were not registered in school; he feared they were truant.

For those relatives who are simply ignorant of home education, one can offer them books or articles to read. If they are open minded, they may eventually support their relative's choice, or at least not actively oppose it. The same applies to neighbors who take umbrage with a family's choice.

When a person who questions home schooling is sincere in her questioning, and open to learning more about the issue, a parent does well to assist her. When the questioner is a faultfinder, lacking an open mind on the subject and only interested in discrediting it, the less said the better.

As Director of Clonlara School, I caution parents and students to make it easy for school officials. Use the words, "enrolled in a private school" first when introducing themselves. It allows the official time to get accustomed to the idea of home education. A large part of the fear that a principle, a superintendent, a counselor, or a teacher has is that a student educated primarily at home will have no records. No cumulative file folder. No test results. No student transcripts (for high schoolers). Putting the best foot forward by revealing that the student was enrolled in a private school as a supplement to home schooling puts the official's mind at ease.

What can parents do who choose not to enroll? They can take as much hard evidence as possible with them when they seek to place a student in public school. Cartons of the educational materials used in the home, photos of a student's art accomplishments, any written product that a student may have, documentation of classes the student attended at a community college or elsewhere—these assure the official that the student was seriously pursuing an education. Many students create a portfolio of their work and add to it during each of the high school years. Explanations abut apprenticeships or mentorships—anything that a student did ought all to be there.

When dealing with college admissions officers, students and parents do well to submit a listing of all classes completed and an evaluation of the student's work in the classes. This is called a student transcript. The portfolio (if any) can also be submitted. It need contain only samples of what the student actually did, lest it become too large and unwieldy. Having letters of recommendation from respected community members (a teacher friend, a pastor, etc.) is, yet again, a reassurance to the official that the student is a serious scholar.

One thing that a family ought to do early on in their home educating is to introduce themselves to their state and federal senators and representatives. These individuals usually have local teas or other occasions to meet their constituents. Letting them know that you reside in the district and are active in the political process (if you are) allows them to get the correct impression of home educators: They are reasonably intelligent parents who opt to teach their own youngsters at home in favor of sending them to an institution. This goes a long way toward educating the politicians, and it may help that person make good choices when legislation is introduced and that could impact on home education. These are people who are very familiar with institutional schools, most of which have state and national lobbyists. Home educators are themselves walking, talking advocates of parental choice at its best (and of education at its best, most would agree).

As I see it, parents who are respectful, who act from a position of equality when dealing with any outside officials, are helping both the officials and themselves. It is the children who benefit most, all told.

Chapter 5

How Do I Cope with the Rest of the World?

"Children who are forced to eat acquire a loathing for food and children who are forced to learn acquire a loathing for knowledge."

~ Bertrand Russell
English philosopher and historian

What happens when someone else in your world doesn't support your homeschooling? What if they think you are crazy, delusional, neglectful or just plain wrong? There are ways to cope based on who it is that's making life difficult. Remember, however, that no matter if you are dealing with a grumpy spouse or an intrusive neighbor, the one element that will help convince all of them that homeschooling is the right decision for your family is your overall attitude of confidence and conviction. If you remain strong and sure in what you think of best for your children, you are almost assuredly going to rub off on others and help the entire process.

What if my spouse doesn't want to homeschool?

This will be the biggest problem of the bunch. Let's face it, if your third cousin twice removed doesn't want you to homeschool, you can blow it off and walk away. But if your partner, your spouse, doesn't want to do it, there could be some trouble straight ahead. Can you homeschool without his or her support or blessing? It's possible, but it isn't probable, and it certainly won't be enjoyable for anyone.

The key to solving this dilemma is to find out exactly what it is that your partner is objecting to. It is very, very unlikely the entire concept of homeschooling; that's too broad and too vague. Talk with each other and find out the precise reason he or she is reluctant. Perhaps your wife doesn't want to homeschool because she doesn't feel capable of the job or because she is afraid it will take up so much time that she will have to sacrifice other aspects of her life to do it. Maybe your husband doesn't want to homeschool because he thinks it is an inferior education or that it will cost too much. No matter what the specific issue is, the first step to resolving it is pinpointing it; then you can work together to see if it can be resolved.

How do you handle the other conflicts that come up within your relationship? Do you talk things over, make lists, get quiet and think, do some research, talk to others? Whatever method has worked best for you in the past is most likely going to be the one that will work for you both now.

No matter what your partner's main objection to home education is, there are ways to learn more about it that can lead to a resolution. If money is the concern, for example, spend some time talking to homeschoolers, looking through catalogs and coming up with a basic figure of what you think it will all cost. (Most likely, your estimate will be high, since beginning homeschoolers often think they need more than they actually do.) Show your partner this figure and talk about how it can be merged into the budget. Putting real numbers to worries can frequently dispel the fear. The same will work if the concern is time; talk to others, read some books and figure out how much time you think homeschooling will take each day (once again, your estimate is probably going to be too high). Then, together, look at how that amount of time can be handled on a daily basis. Many times it won't entail huge lifestyle changes but perhaps just getting up a little earlier, spending a little less time on other things and sharing chores and other responsibilities.

As a team, write down what elements within homeschooling are causing one of you difficulty, and then list the ways each one can be addressed. Often the answer lies in just doing a little reading and a little research.

Here are some other ways to help:
- Read a wide variety of books about homeschooling.
- Attend local homeschool meetings together and meet other homeschoolers.
- Attend a homeschooling conference together.
- Agree to homeschool on a temporary or trial basis, and then evaluate it to see how each person is doing or feeling.

Like any other difficult issue that comes up in a relationship, the key to working this problem out lies in keeping communication between both of you open and friendly. Work hard to understand each other's viewpoints; listen to each other's opinions; be willing to discuss the same things again and again until you start to make some progress; be flexible enough to do some compromising if it means you come closer to an agreement. Homeschooling is family project; it takes cooperation, encouragement and support from everyone. Without your spouse's approval, you are in an uphill race that just might take too much effort for you to finish. If you remember that both of you really do have the same goal—the best possible education and life for your child(ren)—then you can come closer to sharing the same pathway to that goal.

What about unhappy grandparents and other relatives?

Perhaps the best way to keep your cool when your parents or other relatives start to express their unhappiness over your homeschooling decision (sometimes loudly and repeatedly; sometime subtly and annoyingly) is to remember their true motivation. It isn't to make you gray before your time; it's not to make you dread their visits or phone calls—it's because they also love your children deeply, and they are concerned that perhaps your decision isn't in their grandchildren's (or nephew's/niece's/cousin's) best interests.

Once more, the key to solving this problem is in finding out precisely what it is about homeschooling that worries your relatives and then addressing that particular concern in much the same ways you would with a negative spouse. Many times, the entire conflict can be solved through two simple steps: communication and involvement. Welcome their questions (if they're asked nicely; you should insist on no rudeness) and hopefully, they will then welcome your answers.

Involve them in your children's education if you can, invite them to a homeschool- ing meeting; take them along on a field trip; have them come and visit and teach a class or two to your kids. Often just seeing what you are doing with your children, seeing that you are actively involved and that you are not letting their minds rot in front of the television for 14 hours a day, can allay many of their fears. Show them the story your son wrote or the model your daughter put together. By giving them this glimpse into what your family's homeschooling truly is, many of their concerns about socialization and/or academics will lessen, if not disappear altogether.

Many times, once a dialogue is started, you may well discover that the main reason they are upset about your homeschooling decision is that they perceive it as an implied criticism of their long-ago choice of public education for you or your spouse. While you are actually rejecting public education, they may feel you are rejecting *them* for choosing that very same public education. They may see your decision as a judgment on them. While you may fervently wish that you too had been given the chance to be homeschooled, most of us recognize that our parents did the best they could for us and that home education was simply unknown when we were children. There is no blame there—something grandparents should be told in case this is what they are feeling.

If, however, no matter what you say or try to do, you find that these relatives are not coming around and are, in fact, undermining your position with your children by asking questions like, "Don't you wish Mommy or Daddy would let you go to school?" or "Aren't you sad to be missing all the fun of school?", then it is time to take off the nice hat and put on the protective one. Insist that they not make comments like that to your children. If they have an issue, they can take it up with you or stay quiet. If they refuse, consider limiting their access to your children.

What about nosey neighbors and other nuisances?

Sometimes the majority of the unpleasant comments and questions you and your children encounter will come from people that aren't close to you or even complete strangers, like store clerks or co-workers. How much you choose to tell them or how you choose to respond to their words is up to you. How important is this person to you? Is it someone you or your kids have to deal with on a somewhat regular basis? If so, you might want to invest more time and attention to your responses than you will when responding to the lady behind you in the grocery store. As Susan Evans wrote, "In the end, consider where your obligations lie. Are you obliged to keep the neighbors and relatives stress-free or to raise your children the best way you know?"

In Borg Hendrickson's book *Homeschooling: Taking the First Step*, he responds to the question of how to deal with disapproving people this way: "Smile. Just smile . . your own homeschooled children will eventually be your live evidence." Believe it or not, you will find that many of your most harsh critics, if enough time and information is involved, will become your strongest supporters of all. It isn't uncommon for grandparents who once despaired at the idea of their grandkids being homeschooled to regale their friends and neighbors with how smart, kind, mature and wonderful these children are now and isn't homeschooling wonderful?!

What happens if my child doesn't want to homeschool?

While many children love the idea of homeschooling, especially if they have been in a stressful or negative school situation already, there are some who may object to your decision. Don't ignore this and don't think it will just go away. If your child isn't behind this decision, there is going to be a lot of stress and unhappiness for everyone in the family.

Once again, the key to this dilemma is in finding out exactly what your child is objecting to. Is he afraid he won't be able to play basketball anymore? Is she upset that she isn't going to be able to see her friends? Any objection your child has is bound to have some merit, and although it may seem somewhat trivial to you, it most likely is not remotely trivial to your child.

Start by talking about how your child feels. List the questions, worries, concerns and objections, and then address each one. If she is afraid that she won't be able to see her friends, show her the different ways they can still stay in contact and get together on a regular basis. If he is afraid he won't get to play ball, find other places to play or call the school and see if he can still be part of the team (schools vary on their policies of allowing homeschooled students to be involved in extracurricular activities). Make a list of other ways to get fun and friends in (socialization is almost always a child's main objection to homeschooling) like 4H, Boy/Girl Scouts, the YMCA, church, youth groups and of course, all the kids in local homeschooling groups.

Involve your child in the homeschooling plan. Talk about all of the reasons why you made this decision; it's important that he understand your motives and your thoughts. Shift the focus from what she isn't going to be able to do to what she is going to be able to do as a result of homeschooling. Brainstorm on what she might want to learn and places he might want to go. Be willing to propose a compromise: if your child will try homeschooling for six months, for example, you will be open to the option of putting him back into school.

Point out what they won't have to cope with when homeschooling. Did he hate to ride the bus? Did she hate taking showers after P.E. with all the other girls? Did he keep falling behind in math class? Did she get threatened in the girl's bathroom? No problem anymore. No more rushing out of the house in the morning for him to catch the bus; no more dealing with the teacher that just never seemed to like her. Get excited at the possibilities that are opening up on this grand new adventure. In time, your recalcitrant child may just become your staunchest fan.

How do I cope with the questions everyone seems to ask?

Even though homeschooling is in the news and certainly becoming more common, it seems like people continue to ask the same questions when they meet homeschoolers. For some, especially young children, these questions are uncomfortable. Some families have been known to carry around a sheet with typical homeschooling answers on it and when people start to question them more than usual, they hand them a copy and, with a polite smile, walk away.

Here are some of the most common questions you or your children will be asked and some of the answers you can use:

- *What grade are you in?* For some families, this is an easy question. If they are following a more structured format, they know the answer. However, for unschoolers, or those close to being unschoolers, this is a toughie. A child may be in sixth grade in math, ninth in reading and third in science or vice versa. If so, how can they answer the question honestly? Options include saying their age instead of their grade or a simple, "It depends on the subject." Old homeschoolers have been known to have more flippant answers like, "I'm a student of life so I have no grade."

- *Don't you miss _____ (fill in the blank)?* This can vary from the prom to being around your peers all day to getting out of the house every day to name just a few. The problem with this question is that it indirectly implies that the child is missing out on something wonderful, and isn't that a shame? Some homeschoolers have the wherewithal to counter the question with a list of all the amazing things they are doing, so they don't have time to miss the _____, but others who have just been withdrawn from school or who are simply shy may find this question quite upsetting.

- *What school do you go to?* While many kids are used to being asked this question when they are out and about during the day, it still can present a dilemma for them. If they reply "I go to homeschool," they know that they are probably going to be asked a lot more questions which they may or may not want to take the time to answer. One solution that works for many homeschooling families is to give their homeschool an actual name and then the child can answer with that. It also comes in handy for older homeschoolers who are filling out job applications and other forms. You can also use it on letterhead paper when ordering materials. You can name your school whatever you want; the more "official" it sounds, the fewer questions you are apt to be asked. You can put your name in the title or use your address and combine it with words like school, academy or institution.

• *What curriculum do you use at home?* Again, for some, this is a no-brainer since these families already use a set curriculum in their homeschooling. All they have to do in this case is whip out the name of it and they are set. For others, it's difficult because they use a combination of materials that are difficult to list or pinpoint. Often the actual answer to this question involves more information than the listener really wants to know. Typical answers range from "A mixture of this and that" to "A little of everything" to the more facetious (albeit honest) "Life is my curriculum."

• *Don't you get tired of being with your kids/parents all day? Don't you wish you could be with people your own age more often?* This is really a pretty intrusive question, but you may well hear it asked anyway. How you answer it depends on how involved you want to get. Some parents simply state that they love their children, so of course they do not get tired of them. They often go on to list all the many, many activities their children are involved in; rarely is there a homeschooled child who doesn't get a chance to be with friends, public or homeschooled. It can be great fun to watch someone's face when a homeschooled child handles this question and surprises others as they rattle off the different things they do in the course of any given week.

How do I deal with hostile or negative school personnel?

Fortunately, encounters with truly hostile school people are not that common. For the most part, public school administrators are familiar with homeschooling and are, ever so slowly, becoming more accepting and supportive of it. However, there are always exceptions, and there are certainly teachers and principals who view homeschooling families as both a threat and an insult and they can make life difficult.

Pat Montgomery, the founder and president of Clonlara Home Based Learning, has excellent advice for parents who are in contact with school personnel: Do your homework. Before you open your mouth or sign a paper, know EXACTLY what your legal rights and requirements are and stick to them like super glue. Know what you have to do, say, and provide, and don't move an inch past that.

Fulfill the law and then just stop. Be polite (remember—you may want to enroll your child in a class or use the school's facilities sometime in the future) but be careful. Borg Hendrickson wrote, "Program yourself to be firmly, persistently, but calmly diplomatic."

If you do have to deal with the school system, do it in writing it at all possible. Avoid the phone and certainly avoid one-on-one encounters. Keep copies of all correspondence you send or receive. If you are required to answer questions, make sure the questions and your answers are written down. Send your mail with a Return Receipt Requested so that you know it was delivered. This may sound distrustful, but it is the best way to protect your family in the long run.

It you aren't sure who to talk to or what to say or you have some questions about contact with the school system in your area, start by talking to other homeschoolers you have met and get their opinions. Often they can help you with hints and tips you might not have otherwise known and perhaps save you some grief.

Lastly—but certainly most importantly—do not be intimidated by public school personnel. Remember that you are not asking for their permission to homeschool your children; they are *your* children and this is your legal right. You are the one in control and with the power to make this educational decision. Even if they disagree and caution you that you are making a mistake, remember that this is your child, your right and your decision. No school official can change that.

In the Trenches

A Unique Opportunity ~ Carolyn Hoagland

Families educating their children without public school have a unique opportunity to think about how children learn to understand themselves and how they come to know what they want and like. When parents and children spend a lot of time together, the parent sees and experiences many of the same things the child does. The child's questions about those experiences can get answered in a relaxed way that comes from having no deadlines and having no need to accommodate a large group of other children while the question is explored.

Compare, for example, the typical nature walk a third grade glass might take, to the spontaneous outdoor walk that can happen often in a family setting. The difference in quality and quantity is obvious. The spontaneous walk is more likely done just for the enjoyment of being outside, to notice how things have changed. Family members may comment how the "oak buds look like red felt today," or a child may ask, "Does the pocket guide have a picture of these leaves that look like mittens?" or "Why does that squirrel jerk his tail like that?" The classroom trip, on the other hand, is probably designed with an objective in mind, perhaps collecting different types of leaves and identifying trees. Consider the result of an intense desire of a child to study a squirrel's actions instead. You can almost hear the teacher yelling, "Henry! Why are you chasing that squirrel!? I don't see any leaves in your hand!" The assumption that tree taxonomy is more important than squirrel behavior is the direct result of the limited amount of time scheduled for the event; there simply isn't time to do both. The teacher may even get the erroneous idea that Henry isn't interested in trees, when he is simply expressing a preference for squirrels at the moment. My guess is that most teachers would like to allow such a child to enjoy observing the squirrel without comment or rebuke, but administrative pressures and curriculum demands require him/her to keep everyone "on task" as much as possible.

Compulsory school attendance, school commuting, and homework devour about 20,000 hours of a child's life. This might be a fair trade if it produced a citizen in possession of a useful trade, an ability and desire to learn new things, and critical thinking skills. But, as many businesses are quick to point out, many high school graduates are barely employable. John Taylor Gatto, a New York State Teacher of the Year and author, has written, "Reading, writing and arithmetic only take about 100 hours to transmit as long as the audience is eager and willing to learn. The trick is to wait until someone asks and then move on fast while the mood is on." The problem with moving children through a predetermined curriculum in age-based herds is that you can't wait until they ask. There is much valuable material to be covered at least three years in a row so that the slower, middle, and faster learners all get a chance to absorb it when they are able and ready. In addition, there are a host of administrative events that distract from actual learning. There are lines to stand in, forms to fill out, and tests to take and grade. The sheer volume of students to be processed changes the nature of the learning event. One or two adults cannot safely take a group of 20 children to a large park without assuming the roll of drill sergeants. "Everyone get in line! Let's stay together. Don't go over by the bushes or get near the creek!"—even though that is probably the most interesting part of the park.

It almost seems as though one of the goals of compulsory schooling is the crippling of true initiative. Compulsory schooling rewards the kind of initiative that stays within the lesson plan and daily schedule. When people admonish me that my own children must "Go to school, learn to take orders or how else will they ever get a job?", I find myself asking are those really my goals for my children? What I hear in that admonishment is a well-trained person who has been conditioned to believe that it is better to be secure than satisfied (as though they were mutually exclusive!) As a self-employed computer programmer, I've learned that my security depends on listening to people's problems, estimating a solution, and then following through—finding that solution—no matter what it takes. In public school, children are rarely given the chance to back track and try a different approach when they fail.

One thing that is stymied during those 20,000 hours is the development of self-discipline. When most of your waking hours are watched, planned, graded, and measured, there isn't much time to get into the thousands of little, troublesome situations that require creative solutions. Self-knowledge comes from experiencing an open-ended problem, creating a solution, and then reflecting on the outcome and consequences of your earlier actions. The truthfulness of the words written in a journal about a personal failure has a different impact than a required essay about a successful or "planned to succeed" experiment to be read aloud in front of the class.

The drain of hours spent on compulsory schooling may also prevent community service and household chores. Sullen narcissism is the logical outcome of a situation where everything is done for the child and nothing is asked or required in return. All people, even young, short ones, seek the kind of respect that comes from contributing to the group in a way that is public and undeniable. Self-esteem is the logical outcome of successfully completing a task when your help is truly needed. The process of completing a variety of chores and community service tasks is a good start on the questions of "What do I like?" and "How can I make a difference?"

When I began educating my children without public school, I looked forward to controlling their lives in order to shelter them and ease their transition into the wider world. It didn't take long to realize the impossibility and error of that idea. I should have known better. I had just finished growing some plants from seed and had accidentally left some exposed to a draft in the greenhouse. Buffeted by the rush of fresh air coming in, they developed roots and stems that were twice as thick and strong as the pampered plants. At transplant time, they began growing immediately, while the sheltered plants took several weeks to adjust from the shock of transplanting. Children require a similar experience in their community in order to develop their own sturdy disposition, one that can bend and isn't shocked by new situations.

My state, Tennessee, requires parents to provide four hours of instruction for 180 days per year. The state does not tell us what subjects are to be taught, or which methods to use. Because our children are still in grade school, we find that reading, writing, and arithmetic are easily covered in two hours per day. That leaves another two hours for the arts, history, science, and physical activities. Our best use of this flexible schedule is getting out into the community to engage in apprenticeships, to explore the local landscape, and to follow adults around and see what they do all day and to help whenever possible. Some adult routines will be so immediately boring or distasteful to one of the children that he/she will know in an instant they could never make a living that way.

The child who dreams of becoming a forest ranger may decide differently after being caught outside in a storm and having to walk through several miles of wet, soggy forest in order to get home and into dry clothes. A math hater may develop an intense desire in that direction after 15 minutes of programming and operating a Computer Numerically Control Led milling machine under the direction of a skilled tool and die maker. The young rider who dreams of being a jockey may learn that cleaning out a stable isn't half bad if you get a free riding lesson afterwards. The child who begrudgingly attends a political rally or demonstration may see a different law-making process than the one diagrammed in a social studies textbook.

Most teens go through a period of questing—comparing what they feel to what someone else dictates they should want to learn or do. Yet, their questing is limited by their experience. Do they enjoy growing food, doing legal research, composing music, building long chain polymers, observing animals, or making prosthetic devices for injured persons? How many of these things have they had an opportunity to experience? If most families who educate their children without sending them to school use about four hours a day to get through the "book learning" part of their educational goals, that leaves about 12,000 hours of free time for self-directed experiments, apprenticeships, and service to the community.

Voices of Experience

When Methods Collide ~ Teri Brown

I never even saw it coming. While the children and I were happily unschooling through our days, a train was coming inexorably down the pike that would change our lives forever.

The train was my husband, and the collision was his inability to come to terms with unschooling, his coming face-to-face with my natural learning philosophies. The wreck would leave us stunned and groping for new ways to reach out to each other. Amid the wreckage the entire family would learn what compromise, diplomacy, and love really mean.

Okay, it wasn't quite that dramatic, but it would change how school was conducted in the Brown household. My husband has always been supportive of homeschooling and very interested in the unschooling philosophy. He listened intently as I waxed poetic on the beauty of natural learning and admitted that our children were indeed learning every day. For several years things went beautifully. We were busy educating ourselves, chasing interests, and living our lives. While we were doing that, my husband was watching—both proud of our progress, and worrying about all that he felt we were missing.

Finally after dropping a few hints here and there, it all came out. He wasn't satisfied with the children's education, he felt there were gaps and strongly felt that there are things you need to learn whether you want to or not. Period.

I felt as if the wind had been knocked out of me. Not only was I a confirmed unschooler, I had even written a book on the subject! Now, here my husband was telling me that he couldn't stand behind our unschooling any longer—something had to give.

A word about my husband here—he is not an overbearing, over-structured fanatic. He is an organized, disciplined person who wants the very best for his children. He is almost as educated on homeschooling methods as I am. While he believes unschooling to be a fascinating philosophy with some merit, he is not prepared to "gamble" with our children's entire life. He is far more conventional than I am, and unschooling is just too radical.

So there we were. Stuck between a rock and a hard place where diverse viewpoints meet, and we were unsure of where to go next. I couldn't just ignore his concerns; he is my husband the children's father. In this, as in most of marriage, one person cannot just toss their head and do what they want no matter what. Not and have a good marriage anyway!

So we did what most loving couples do when faced with the unknown. We argued. Now my dear husband and I love a good argument. We learned long ago how to do it without going for the jugular. Our concerns were brought out in the open and analyzed. Reasoning, logic, and tradition were all discussed. Intensely at times, but honestly.

We finally decided to have a summit meeting, a meeting where east meets west, where radical meets conventional, where—you get the idea! Off to Starbucks we went (isn't that where all important meetings take place?). We each wrote out a few sentences of our different philosophies. Why was it important to him for our children to have more structure to their education, and why was it important for me to unschool them?

Addressing these things, we began to compromise. "What is important for them to know?" I remember asking. "If you were to list three things you feel they absolutely have to learn, what would they be?"

"Besides fishing, changing the oil in your car, and how to order a good café latte? I would have to say, spelling, reading comprehension, and consumer math." My husband the comedian.

"Reading comprehension can be learned by living," I argued. "Following a recipe, learning to play a game, and talking about your favorite books are all exercises in reading comprehension."

He conceded that they were.

But what about consumer math?" He countered. "Our children are good at the consuming part, not so good at the math part." He had a point.

"How much time?" I asked. "How much time constitutes being educated to you?"

He snorted, far too wise to fall into that trap! "You know their learning styles better, what do you think?"

"A half an hour, twice a week?" I asked hopefully.

"Two hours a day, five days a week."

HA! Like that was going to happen. Little by little, bit by bit, we reached compromises and understanding. This is how we worked it out.

Since the children had already made educational goals for themselves, I would use those to make some of the changes that were important to my husband. In order to preserve their own independence, I make up books that have each day's activities in it, along with almost everything they need in order to accomplish them. I used a unit study approach using books they were interested in reading, and from that, I was able to pull together quite a bit of subject matter in a few well-chosen activities.

In our weekly schedule, I set aside five hours a week for "book work" (gritting my teeth a little here" and another two for educational games that are a take off on their own work. Following some of the thoughts of John Taylor Gatto, I am setting aside several hours (they don't have a full day) for volunteer work of some sort. I wish we had family closer so they could spend more time with their family as well, as I believe that is an integral part of education.

So there it is. Does that mean we are un-unschooling? I don't think so. I still consider myself and my family as being unschooler—for the most part. We all compromise, make adjustments, and otherwise adapt to the needs of those we love. When differing educational philosophies or parental styles start to create problems, a functional family finds a way to make it work. One of the beauties of educating your children at home is the time you have to find out what works best for everyone involved. And that includes the parents. That is just a part of being a family.

Teri Brown is a former homeschooling mom and author and has a young adult novel called *Read My Lips* coming out in summer 2008.

Chapter 6

What About The Teen Years?

"They will say you are on the wrong road if it is your own."

~ Antonio Porchia, Spanish author

Ah, the teen years.

Sigh.

When I wrote this book in 2001, I only had one teenager. She was 17 and she was already teaching me how very little I knew about teenagers. Flash forward to today and I have two teenagers in the house (the oldest is 23 now).

I'm still learning, believe me. Each one of them has had such a distinctly different response to becoming a teenager that every time I think I know what to expect, I am wrong... again.

Sigh.

If there is life on other planets, I imagine that even those alien creatures must sigh when puberty hits. The teenage years can be tough for each person in the family but how tough and how bad can vary greatly from family to family. Does homeschooling stop all that teenage angst? No. Do homeschooled teens stop thinking that the entire world revolves around them and that mom and dad are pretty clueless how about life REALLY is? No. Will homeschooling protect them from depression, anger, dissatisfaction, loneliness and confusion? Don't I wish, but no.

Can homeschooling make these teenage days a little easier? Yes. Can it help put a buffer—not a shield—between teens and the dangers of drugs, alcohol and pregnancy? Yes. Can it keep you both a little closer so that this time doesn't so much about breaking away as in letting go? Yes. There are no guarantees, of course. After all, there is a lot of logic in the quote, "Raising teenagers is like trying to nail Jell-o® to a tree."

Teens will still waffle between child and adult; they will struggle to find their places in the world and will still look at you now and then like you are not too bright. However, homeschooling can also give your teens a chance to excel in the world at a time when it is most needed. It is a time when these kids are so emotionally vulnerable, afraid to look into the unknown future and yet so compelled to, when their desires outweigh their expertise, their income and their abilities and it is a time when your presence, whether welcomed or not, is so vital.

Homeschooling a teen is different than the elementary years. Whatever method you have chosen to follow, this period will allow for more autonomy as less time is needed for instruction and follow through, and more is devoted to guidance and support. Please remember that the time you spend listening to them tell you about a best friend that has let them down, a boy at the local video store that flirted with them or a work situation that has challenged them that these moments are just as important—perhaps even more so—than any of the so-called curriculum you are going over together. These are the moments that sustain the bonds through the turbulent times ahead.

How do I teach my teen college-prep material I don't understand myself?

We are fortunately living in an era where the options for education just keep increasing by leaps and bounds. The subjects typically covered in high school can be intimidating for parents; many of us don't remember how to conjugate verbs in French or how trigonometry works. What to do?

First, and most importantly, stop and ask yourself *Does my child really need to know this information?* Think about it. Have you ever used this information in your life? Is this information that will be needed in most work situations or in daily routines? If the answer is yes, then most likely your child will need to know it too. But, if you can't come up with any sensible reason your child needs this specific information right now (other than you/your child's peers learned it at this age—which doesn't count), be willing to discard it.

It's important, as your approach these years, to have a rough idea of whether or not your teen is planning to pursue going to college or some other form of higher education. This can change the slant of your curriculum since most colleges will have some basic requirements. They might, instead, be looking at going directly into a job or vocational school or perhaps their plans are to travel awhile or start their own business. The options are almost limitless. Don't get caught into the notion that the only way to be successful in life is to get a college degree. That isn't true; many, many people have rewarding careers and lives without such a degree. It is only one avenue of many.

This is a slap-in-the-face notion to some people. I've lost count of how many times I have encountered someone, homeschooling and otherwise, who is appalled at my attitude towards college. While I think it is the perfect choice for some, I also heartily support the idea of not going to college and doing something equally worthwhile with one's life. I was once interviewed for a magazine article and the journalist asked me if my oldest had gone/was going to go to college. I said no. He was shocked. He then asked me, "How will she ever be successful then?" Now it was my turn to be shocked. Since when did college equate or guarantee success in life? My response was, "If my daughter has a job that she finds worthwhile, if she loves someone and is loved in return, then in my opinion, she is wonderfully successful." I know I can—and I bet you can—count scads of people you know who have gone on to wonderful lives without a college degree, as well as those who had a degree and it either did nothing to help them find success or was never even utilized because the person went in entirely different directions. As someone recently put it on a blog, "Education is absolutely necessary, but you should never let school interfere with your education." Okay, I'm off my soapbox now.

If you have determined that your teen needs to know certain material, what next? Have you talked to your teen about it? I encourage you to do so. Their input is invaluable and it is their lives we are talking about in the first place. You may discover that your teens have some goals you didn't know a thing about. Together you can brainstorm a kind of curriculum to use or a list of what you want to cover between now and "graduation," and then figure out how you are going to get the material for the subjects you don't feel you personally can cover.

Here are some of the best resources:
- find a local tutor or mentor to teach the subject
- purchase a packaged curriculum for this subject
- see if your spouse/partner feels comfortable covering this subject
- attend a community class on this subject
- take online classes for this subject
- learn the subject right along with your teen
- get another homeschooler to teach the subject
- join an umbrella school that teaches this subject
- talk to relatives, neighbors and co-workers and see if they know the subject well enough to teach it

If you do decide to enroll in an umbrella school, make sure to check their educational philosophy to see if it meshes with yours. Ask about fees and what those fees include and how to contact other enrollees for their opinions and thoughts about the school.

How does my child get a diploma?

The very first thing you need to do when you come up against the idea of a diploma for your child is to repeat to yourself at least ten times: *It is just a piece of paper. It is just a piece of paper.* A diploma truly is just a piece of paper. Have you looked it up in the dictionary lately? While some might believe that it is defined as "a magical piece of paper that allows all high school graduates to find worthwhile jobs and entrances to any high quality college or university," it actually means "a piece of paper signifying the completion of a line or course of study."

A diploma is not a ticket into a better future but simply a piece of paper saying, yep, you are done with this section of education now. Good job. While it is important to have a diploma for some life journeys—the military for example—it doesn't have to be a high school diploma that came from a public or private high school. Job applications often ask if a person has one. No matter where it came from, if you have one, the answer is yes, so check yes. The chances of the employer wanting to see it and read it over are virtually nil. Employees care far more about experience than GPAs. Even the military is beginning to relax its requirements on having one. As for colleges, they depend more on transcripts, test scores, letters of recommendation, resumes, interviews and portfolios than on an actual diploma.

If you still believe you need one, or if a circumstance comes up that demands one, here are some choices you have:

- Make your own. You can get forms from many office supply stores or homeschool catalogs. You can also just create one on your home computer or hire a calligrapher to make an artsy one. If your child has homeschooled through high school and completed the course of study you or they have outlined, then this diploma is completely legitimate. As homeschooling author Cafi Cohen says, "Do homeschoolers need a high school diploma? The answer is sometimes. Do they need a diploma from an accredited school? The experience of thousands of families indicate that the answer is almost never."
- Get a General Equivalency Diploma or GED instead.
- Join an umbrella school. Many provide a diploma as part of their services.
- Enroll in an independent study program. Again, many of them

provide a diploma as part of their services.
- Check with your state DOE. Find out if your state offers state approved diplomas if certain requirements are fulfilled.

Additional ideas about diplomas can be found in Larry and Susan Kaseman's excellent article "Taking Charge" in the March-April, 1998 issue of *Home Education Magazine*. In response to the question of "What can homeschoolers do if a diploma is required?" they wrote:

"Start by asking who is requiring the diploma, for what purpose, whether the requirement could be waived and whether an alternative to a diploma might be acceptable. Diplomas are required in surprisingly few situations. Often it is enough to simply say that you were home- schooled, do not have an official diploma, but are an independent learner with lots of experience asking responsibility for your own learning. Increasingly employers and colleges and universities are seeking and welcoming homeschoolers because of the strong reputation we are developing.

"If a diploma is required for some reason . . . homeschoolers can issue their own diplomas just as other private schools do, by setting up criteria that must be met and awarding diplomas to people who meet them. The question with this kind of diploma is how to make it convincing to whoever needs to be convinced. Sometimes a formal certificate is all that is required. These can be purchased from school supply houses or generated by computer."

What about graduation?

Graduation is a lot like a diploma: it doesn't have to be sponsored by the local public high school to be valid. When your teen completes his course of study (whatever that may mean in your homeschooling perspective), have a graduation ceremony. Rent a hall, open up the backyard, reserve the church, call in that favor with your Aunt Mildred owes you and use her garden. Order a cake, get some music, even find a gown at your local thrift store. Invite friends, family, neighbors, coworkers—anyone else you want and make it a real celebration. Take pictures and grab the video camera. Have speeches. Make a display out of your child's projects, papers and other scholastic achievements.

How do you know when your child is ready to "graduate"? In Cafi

Cohen's article "How Do We Know When We're Done?" (July/Aug 1998 issue of *Home Education Magazine*), she writes, ". . .many homeschooling families decide for themselves what constitutes high school graduation. These families use one or more of the following criteria to set goals and make decisions about finishing high school:
- Local high school diploma requirements
- College recommendations
- Time spent
- Age of the homeschooler
- Ability to support oneself financially
- Teenager's evaluation of his readiness to move on"

What about the prom?

The prom often means far more to us parents than it does to most kids. After all, they have not been exposed to the years of hype that we were in school. It just doesn't have the importance it did to some of us. And for many of us, the prom was not that great an experience anyway. Some of us didn't get invited at all. Some of us did and had a rotten time. Others went and then risked their lives by drinking and driving afterwards. Many lost their virginity that night.

If your teens do want to attend a prom, there are several options. If they are dating a public schooler, they can attend the school's prom. Best of all, they can create one of their own. Homeschooling proms are slowly gaining in popularity. Grace Llewellyn's Not Back to School Camp includes a prom each summer and campers come in everything from formals to duct tape. As one attendee puts it, "People dress up for this dance in very individual ways. One person might have wings on; another might be wearing a 40's style swing skirt with sequins, and there are even people in drag for fun. No one has to worry about who is with whom and what they are wearing or if it's in style or not. We are there with our friends to have fun and that's it."

Cities across the nation are putting together these dances. (For a list, check out http://homeschooling.gomilpitas.com/articles/102303.htm) I have been fortunate enough to be part of Portland's Homeschooling prom. The first year about 75 people came; the second year 110 and this past year 125 or so. My husband and I were head chaperones at the last one and had as much fun hanging out and dancing as many of the kids there. It was held in a lovely downtown ballroom. My eyes were all teary by the end of the evening as I saw my eldest son slow dance with a girl for the first time and my youngest daughter win the award for Most Elegant.

How does my homeschooled teen get a job?

The majority of homeschooled teens have part time jobs because they have big plans for the money they make—be it college, an expensive hobby or perhaps some traveling around to visit friends in other states. The advantage that these teens have is that their schedules are far more flexible than those of their public school counterparts, and this availability makes it easier for them to get hired. Many teen homeschoolers have jobs within their own families' businesses or have even started businesses of their own. It's not unusual to read about homeschooling teens who have their own store, product or service and making a decent income at a relatively early age. The entrepreneurial spirit is often alive and thriving in this group. Others may get your typical teen job: waitress, babysitter, lawn care, fast food worker, etc. Whatever position they get, a job can teach them all about money management, attitude, responsibility and motivation.

As their parents, you might guide them towards choosing some kind of job that relates to their personal interests. If they are thinking about becoming a veterinarian, how about a part time job at a local pet shop? If they are into music, why not apply at the local music store? Of course, make these suggestions very subtly—even homeschooled teens tend to view their parents' recommendations as suspicious.

Before your teens go out on that first job hunt, give them some pointers (refer to subtlety mentioned in above paragraph) about filling out an application. You might brainstorm together on who to put as references and even create a resume to take along. Many homeschooled teens have done enough interesting traveling, volunteering and experimenting that they can create a very impressive resume for potential employers. Because these teens are accustomed to being around adults, they often do an excellent job in interviews also, coming across as mature and confident. Of course, this isn't true for all teens, but quite a few.

If taking on a part time job is not what you or your teen wants at this point in time, consider volunteering on a regular basis instead.

Many of the foremost leaders in the homeschool movement strongly advocate incorporating some kind of community service into a family's overall curriculum because of the important values it can teach a person. Volunteer opportunities can often be found through local nursing homes, humane shelters, community centers, YM/YWCAs, libraries and parks and recreation departments. For other possibilities, check out www.volunteeramerica.com

What about an apprenticeship or internship?

A truly wonderful idea for your teen is an apprenticeship and/or internship. It can help them discover that yes, they love this work and it is their future direction, or no, they can't stand it and it's time to look elsewhere. It gives your teen a taste of the responsibility that comes with a job and the experience just might make them more employable down the road.

Who can you contact for this kind of arrangement? The possibilities are endless but here are some places to get started:
- Friends
- Relatives
- Neighbors
- Coworkers
- Other homeschoolers
- Businesses
- Trade schools
- Career centers
- Search and rescue divisions

Can my homeschooled teen get into college?

The first time I was asked this question was almost 20 years ago (yikes, I feel old!) and I always paused before responding because the answer was tenuous; the truth was it was a challenge. Today, I just smile and say, "No problem." With each passing year, more and more colleges and universities are opening up their doors to homeschoolers. They are finding this new breed of student to be more self-motivated and self-disciplined with a background of rich and varied experiences.

A study was done several years ago about how college admissions officers perceived homeschoolers. When asked how they expected the overall success of homeschooled applicants would compare to traditional high school students during the first year of college, the results listed were:

56%	equally successful
22%	homeschoolers more successful
1%	homeschoolers less successful

To find out more about college's attitudes and thoughts about homeschoolers, access the article "A Study of Admission Officers' Perceptions of and Attitudes Toward Homeschool Students" from the *Journal of College Admission,* available at http://findarticles.com/p/articles/mi_qa3955/is_200410/ai_n9443755/pg_1. Another interesting article is "Family Pupils are Homing in on College" available at http://www.dce.harvard.edu/pubs/alum/2003/12.html.

Experts predict that more than one million homeschooled children will be enrolled in colleges and universities by the end of the decade. More than 1,000 colleges accept homeschoolers, but that number is climbing so quickly, it is easier to start counting the ones who don't. Stanford University's letter sent to homeschooled applicants reads, "Homeschooled students are no longer unusual for us and several are usually admitted and enroll at Stanford each year. . . .We are scrupulously fair in evaluating these applicants and they are not at any disadvantage for admissions process." Marlyn McGrath Lewis, Director of Admissions for Harvard College says, "We receive a good number of candidates every year with all or part of their education from a homeschool background. Homeschooling is broader than some people realize. We are looking for the strongest candidates in the world and we find some of those among homeschoolers."

The application process can often be an area where homeschoolers can shine. Instead of just turning in the traditional high school transcripts, many have been known to turn in impressive portfolios full of letters of recommendation (from teachers, employers, pastors, coaches, tutors, coworkers and other community members), resumes, test scores, writing samples, awards, certificates, projects and essays. All of these things can help to make an excellent impression on college officials. However a word of caution—always make sure you know precisely what the college your teen is applying to requires; sometimes colleges can be persnickety to the point of ridiculousness. For example, in 1999, when homeschooler Rio Benin scored a perfect 1600 on the SATs and won a $20,000 scholarship from Intel, the University of California at San Diego turned Rio down because he didn't have a high school transcript. Rio ended up choosing Harvard instead.

Scholarships are just as available to homeschoolers as to those in public school. The key to success when it comes to getting a scholarship is to make sure your child meets all requirements before he/she applies and then, according to homeschooling author Cafi Cohen, the next thing to do is make a follow up call. "It's the single most important thing to do," she says. "It gets you noticed."

One last note on the subject of college: keep in mind that your independent teen may decide that college is not what he/she wants to do. You may agree; you may strongly disagree. Forcing a child to go to college is rarely a good idea in any family, and with children who have had the freedom of homeschooling, it can be disastrous. When they turn up their noses at your suggestions or the brochures you laid on their desks, stay cool and don't let it become an issue. If that happens, communication often stops completely and anything you have to say is going to fall on deaf ears. They may just need some time off between high school and college. Listen to what they have in mind and remember that they might utilize this time to save money for future education, gain additional career experience, travel, volunteer, be part of a foreign exchange program or take some local college prep classes. There are many choices out there beyond college, and perhaps one of them is just the right one for your teen. By giving them the freedom and trust to make decisions, you may just find that they were right—college wasn't' the best option for them; or, conversely, they may find that you were right and after spreading their wings for a little while, they will pick up the brochures and start asking questions.

What about playing sports, joining the drama club, being in the orchestra and taking driver education?

Let's face it. The public school system is always going to have some kind of program that will interest your kids. You have several options. You can contact the school and see what their policy is on allowing homeschoolers to be on the team or in the class. Some are very open to the concept, while others are reluctant or even hostile. A number of them have school policies in place that simply don't allow for non-students to be enrolled in any of their programs. Of course, you can also encounter other difficulties like my husband and I when our 15 year old daughter (at the time) wanted to take driver education at the school just down the street.

I called and spoke with the teacher of the class. I said, I know how kids are at this age—very cliquish—so could you perhaps make an extra effort for my daughter and perhaps seat her near one of your friendlier students, i.e. not the head cheerleader or the football quarterback who have too many "normal" friends to reach out to someone new? His response, "Sure will!" What did he do? He wrote in the attendance book, next to her name, "Can't make friends easily." That is NOT what I said.

When I called back the following week to say that my daughter came home from class in tears because every time she sat down at a table, the other students moved to other seats, he said, "I will take care of that."

He did.

He put her next to a student with such physical disabilities that he couldn't actually speak. I guess that is what you do with the students who "can't make friends easily." Sigh. In a three page, very eloquent letter to the teacher, my daughter withdrew from the class. I still remember her handing it in to the teacher, who insisted on reading it while she stood there and then, when he asked why she would leave a class that she was making an "A" in, she replied, "How can a person begin to learn when they are surrounded by people that behave like this? Just give me the textbook and I will do it on my own." She got an A-plus that day from us.

If you would prefer to stay away from the public school system altogether (a decision I personally applaud), there are other places that can fulfill many of your teen's interests. If playing sports is their thing, look into the YM/YWCA. Check to see if there are local leagues through businesses or community groups. Perhaps you live in an area with enough homeschoolers to start your own team. Can your teen join the team of a private school in your city? How about personal lessons?

The same holds true for drama and orchestra and choir and art and any of those other classes that require a group. Check with small community theatre groups or the city orchestra. Arrange for private lessons. Look beyond the school as the place for any of these activities.

As for driver's ed (hear me gnashing my teeth?), some schools will allow your teens to come in and take the course (even if they can't make friends easily), but others will not. A teen can be taught by mom and dad but it may mean they have to be over 16 to get their licenses. (Many parents love this delay. More time to mature). There are a number of packaged driver education programs that you can buy online such as Driver Ed in a Box® and national Driver Training Institute. Also check out the driver's ed program available on the excellent site A to Z Homeschooling (http://homeschooling.gomilpitas.com/articles/021599.htm)

Non public schooled driver's ed can affect the discount on some people's car insurance, so be sure and talk to your agent about that. Just remember—like the old song, "Anything the public school can do, we can do better!"

Voices of Youth: Essays by Teens and Young Adults

The decision to homeschool is one of the best things that's ever happened to me; it lets me live. I don't know what I would do otherwise. I can't imagine a life without the choices I have, the freedom and the opportunities. I feel so lucky that I can live this way, without people telling me what and when and how to learn it. Instead my parents encourage me to follow my interests wherever they may lead. To just do it, whatever it is; just go out and live my life. That may mean working at a Montessori preschool for four years, learning how to teach kids while they teach me how to learn, or working at a living history museum where I give tours to school kids, showing them things from the past, and telling stories about how the pioneers lived.

Community theatre is another place my interests have led me. I've worked in almost every aspect of it from backstage hand to stage manager, props, costumes, makeup, and recently, assistant director. I love the adrenaline rush of a show, and how I handle the chaos of it all. This year I might get to be a guest director.

This past fall I was interested in history, so I got to visit some friends out of town and hear Howard Zinn, author of *A People's History of the United States,* speak. My friend and I had a great time reading out loud to each other from his book while we made apple crisp and took breaks to discuss the events of history.

Recently homeschooling gave me the freedom to take a trip down to California to visit my grandparents. My grandma, who's a writer, worked with me on a report about women photographers. My grandpa, an avid photographer, took me on long walks and taught me how to take good pictures. They shared with me their love of photography, writing, art, and their curiosity about life, all things I hope to retain and incorporate into my own life more.

Now I am hoping to take the freedom I have and use it to work on my writing, learning to finish the things I start, and perhaps even getting published occasionally. This essay seems a good beginning, as it is in itself another good example of the opportunities I am given.

When I think back to the two years that I did spend in school, I can't think of anything I miss now. I know that the first year of homeschooling was difficult. At one point I wanted to go back to school. But when my parents and I talked, I realized that the only reason I wanted to go back was for recess. Now I have found a group of friends, much more interesting and varied than I ever had at recess, and I can't think of a single thing I miss about school. In the end, I think the decision to homeschool has been one of the best things in my life. It has provided so many opportunities that I never would have had otherwise. -Elizabeth

There was a point in time when I scoffed at the idea of being homeschooled. I was nine or ten and the thought of not actually physically going to school where my teachers and friends were was somewhat heartbreaking. A year or two went past, and as I began to experience more and more of my public school system, the more the idea of homeschooling began to appeal to me. By the time I was in middle school, I was ready to be rid of the insane insomnia that plagued me weekly, brought on—I'm positive—by my intense loathing of school. This was coming from a kid who once couldn't wait for September when classes would start up again. Clearly, something was wrong; and when coupled with my mom's long time interest in self-education, we all made the decision to start homeschooling both my sister and I.

I know popular belief is that homeschoolers tend to lead a somewhat sheltered lifestyle, and while this is true of a small percentage of homeschoolers, it's certainly one of the biggest urban myths around today. From the time I was 12 years old until I started college in 2000, I was homeschooled, and I led a varied and exciting existence. I was always off somewhere during what were my "high school" years. Whether it was traveling around the country with my mom and sister, volunteering at one of my many places of interest, or attending yet another meeting for a council I was part of, I was never home and never bored.

I had lots of friends. I had boyfriends. I went to regular high school sporting events. I went to regular high school dances, including yes, the senior prom. I went to plays and musicals and conferences and other social events in my area and around the country. I didn't miss out on anything during my homeschooling years except perhaps the harmful peer pressure, or pressure from adults in suits behind desks who had to pretend like they cared about where your life was going after high school when really, you were just another name in the books or more state money in their pockets. To miss out on something, you have to feel like there's a void inside you somewhere that hasn't been filled. I never had that feeling about my schooling or the experiences I had. I can honestly say that while I am sure I could have done more or better, I never felt unfulfilled.

As I've ventured off into the wonderful world of higher education, I've come to realize that my education was far more rounded than the majority of the people I attend college with. My instructors have come to realize that I am not just another shut away, anti-social, puritanical homeschooled production, but rather an individual who has experienced enough to be able to relate to any subject with some clarity and understanding. I can hold an intelligent conversation about the Beatles, or about the pros and cons of RU486, and at the drop of a hat, I can quote you Shakespeare, Weezer, and the Rocky Horror Picture Show.

I couldn't have asked for a better education. The years I spent in public school where beneficial in their own way, and I wouldn't go back to change those if I had the chance. They led to an even greater appreciation of the chance to control my own education once it was thrust into my own two hands, and now that I've had two years to look back on it all, I realize that I had the education of a lifetime.

Now all I need to do is get through this college stuff…

-Cloe Rose

I don't really think I'm missing out on anything at all by not going to school. Except perhaps I miss having to learn things that I'll never remember because they aren't important to me. And I'll miss out on the cliques and worrying about how popular I am. I'll miss out on spending all my daylight hours and then some on schoolwork, and then homework, and then do it again tomorrow.

Instead I'll just have to be content with getting up and going to work all day. I work at a veterinarian's office as an assistant. I've worked on everything from cats and dogs, cows and horses, to tarantulas and camels, otters and eagles. Then when I get off work, I'll maybe go ride my horse and practice for all the shows that I go to in the summer. Or perhaps tonight is one of the nights when I have a TaeKwondo or dance class. Or maybe I'll go home and read.

Right now that would be reading about how to build natural energy sources such as solar power systems or hydro plants or how to build cob houses. I'm also designing a garden for our house and to go along with it, I'm reading about medicinal herbs. As long as we're going to have a garden, we might as well grow some herbs that will do us some good. Plus it's just nice to know what's edible when I'm out in the mountains hiking or camping, which I do a lot of, and get hungry or feel like munching on something.

Perhaps I could learn some things from school, but I wouldn't learn them as well nor would they stay learned as well. One of the best things that ever happened in my life was quitting school at the age of nine or so and becoming an Unschooler. Since then I have had more practical and hands-on learning than I ever had in my first three years of school. Since rising out of school, I have moved away from the city, helped build our straw bale and timber frame house; I've worked as a dog walker for our humane society, as a grocery stocker, helped do janitorial work at a grocery store, worked on a horse ranch and learned to ride, washed dishes and been a back up cook at a small restaurant in town, and now I am working with the veterinarian.

And so I would say that for me, Unschooling is the best choice there is, although for others, school may be more their style. I think of unschooling as more of a state of mind than of a state of not going to "school." An Unschooler is someone who wants to learn; someone who will look beyond the conventional learning atmosphere and seek out people who know the things they want to learn, and to learn from those people or libraries or the nighttime sky. Unschoolers never stop learning because they realize that they learn from everything they ever do, and that they will only stop doing things, even so much as just watching the birds, when they die.
-Ruth

When the word "homeschooling" entered my vocabulary, my life began again. Like any new project you start, the beginning is shaky, nervous, and unsure. At the beginning of my homeschooling career, I decided to sit for a while at the starting line. I felt the traumatic "missing out syndrome" several times, with my friends all excited about proms and worried about schoolwork. I was staring down a blank and yet incredibly exciting path. I think that when you are told only one way, and then you realize there is a different way, and make the conscious decision to choose that different way, a way that calls to you but yet is much less traveled, your heart can skip a beat or two. It wasn't until I became immersed in my new way, my new and different path, that the world opened up to me. For the first time since I was a child, I saw the tremendous beauty and endless options. The first six months to a year after I quit school, I knew no other unschoolers in real flesh and blood and hanging out with my high school friends seemed easy and familiar.

It was a slow transformation, and as my interests took me over, my path unfolded before me. I decided to become a vegetarian and quickly found an organization dedicated to teaching people how to become one. I jumped onboard their Core Team and started helping and meeting lots of people in my area who believed in the same things I did. I wanted to dance and found a swing dance troop and learned not only about Haitian dance and movement, but about the people and culture of Haiti. I was interested in sculpture and art, so I took a sculpture class at the local junior college and found an amazing teacher. The list continued as my true interests sparked and were finally set free. I no longer gained anything from drinking beer with my "friends," and I actually wanted to share my story with the adults who thought I was either a genius, a drop out, or on medication.

Homeschooling has given me a path with a big, bright light everywhere that school never gave me. I imagine that if everyone, especially every teenager, was given the choice to go to school, we, as teenagers, would have more self-confidence than most 40-year-old adults. Once you begin to work towards a goal you set for yourself, instead of a goal that your parents and/or society has set for you, your eyes see life the way it really is, as you make it!

-Danielle

Homeschooling has allowed me the free time to pursue my interests. I enjoy drawing, particularly fantasy and animals. I wrote a novel last year. Writing is my second-favorite hobby. I write and illustrate many stories. My hope is to someday be either an author or illustrator.

Learning outside school has been really enjoyable. I like the small class and the fact that I can hug my teacher. The hours are user-friendly, and there's always time to pursue your biggest interest, whatever it may be. Mine change frequently.

I've recently begun teaching myself HTML. It's challenging, but I've learned how to find resources and ask questions, and I'm making progress. It's good to be able to just decide to learn something and have the time to pursue it as long as I want to.

Another thing about homeschooling that is particularly enjoyable is the reaction from people in public places. When I was younger, I sometimes heard "No school today?" as I stood at the grocery store checkout lane with my mother.

I used to answer "No, I'm homeschooled," and give them my winning, I'm-such-a-cute-7-year-old smile. It was particularly successful when I was missing my front teeth. For some reason, adults think that's cute.

No one really asks anymore, though. I think there are many more kids being homeschooled now than there were when I was a kid. When I'm out and about, I see many families with children, shopping in the grocery store, at the library or just out for a walk.

~ Alyssa

From 2001: After seven years of having been enrolled in school, it was easy to see that homeschooling helps to open one's mind more so than conventional schooling. It seems to encourage people to search out knowledge in their own ways. I've noticed that most homeschooling and unschooling families encourage learning whatever interests the child, opening doors for that person whenever possible. When anyone sets out to do something that they want to do, rather than something being forced upon them, the mind is immediately more open and accepting towards the information being presented.

While in school, I found it to be somewhat "numbing." Conventional schooling presses a strict curriculum and a "don't ask, don't tell" attitude. Kids are told to do a set amount of work and are graded on it. However, the average person in school lacks massive amounts of motivation so they often just do the bare minimum. The only motivation there is the desire not to get into trouble or get detention. They do just enough to get by.

Since I have been out of school, I have been able to pursue things that I enjoy more than textbook learning. I was able to learn how to cook, hold a steady job on "school days," learn photography, and take art classes that a school would not be able to provide. These things were so much easier to learn than anything in school because I wanted to be there and I wanted to learn them. My mind just seemed to grasp things easier.

I've seen that homeschooling can open doors towards the world and towards careers more than traditional schooling. I know future writers and performers and people that don't know what they want to do yet, but are trying everything just for the experience. We have all been finding things that we love and things to learn, despite not having someone shoving assignments down our throats. We still learn tons—just not in a conventional way.

From 2007: I just quit my job. It was hard. In fact, all day I've felt sick to my stomach just knowing that at the end of the day, I would sit down at the work computer and write my boss an email titled "Three Week Notice." Quitting jobs is as hard for me as breaking up with someone. The first time I broke up with a girl, I almost passed out. Another time, I threw up and another time, I felt very similar to how I've felt today except now I have a pint of beer to soothe me.

The first time I quit a job, I was almost 17 and had been working there for a little over three years. It was my first job and I started when I was 13. My mom had been waiting tables at a breakfast restaurant and they needed a dishwasher. She came home one day and asked me if I would like to work as part of my "schooling," and I was more than eager. After not more than two months, the owner/cook asked me if I was comfortable using a knife… and thus began my cooking education. At this point, I've cooked a little of everything—breakfast, lunch and dinner, everything from cheap pizza to filet mignon. When I quit that first job—my boss cried. It's stuck with me. Maybe that makes it harder actually—I never had to watch my ex-girlfriends cry.

But I've finally quit this job, the one I've had for so long now, this job that was supposed to be temporary and then just went bad. All of a sudden, I was making enough money that finding a new job was hard because that could mean a pay cut, and I was already creating a life based on the size of those paychecks. But now I'm finally moving on. I got a job managing the kitchen of a brew pub down the street from my house. I might add that I received this job without my conventional schooling ever being discussed—I got it based solely on experience.

If I hadn't seen you in six years and we sat down to catch up with all that semi-awkward idle chit-chat and you thought homeschooling would be a hurdle for someone to get past, you would be proud of me. But the fact is—it's not a hurdle. You wouldn't be able to tell whether I went to school or not. You would learn that I've created a great life for myself and that my parents are proud of me. I've moved several states away from home and made a life for myself that first and foremost includes my amazing wife of four years—that just so happens to be the author's oldest daughter, Jasmine. I've also legally changed my name. We live in a duplex in a great neighborhood and now I'm only going to be four blocks from work. I have a garden that is still producing tomatoes in mid-October. We have the best dog you've ever known, a fat black lab named Hunter. We just got back from a two week paid vacation and now we're talking about buying a house. It's true that life could be great even if I went to school but it wouldn't be *this* life and I've grown rather fond of it.
-Metro

Yesterday, my youngest brother said something very profound to me. He said, "If something's funky all by itself, then it's just funky. If everything around it's funky, then it's just normal." I see homeschooling in much the same light. It's not right for everybody. Some people feel very at home when they're getting all their education at home, and some feel they can't get all of what they need out of it.

A large advantage I have found with homeschooling is that it made me love learning. Most homeschooled teens and kids can agree with this. I see a lot of public schooled kids and it seems none of them "enjoy" receiving their education. They can't wait to leave school at the end of the day, and dread Monday's, when it all begins again. I know I speak for at least some of the home-learners out there, when I say I never consider homeschooling a chore. It's never something I dread. I remember things more from homeschooling, than I think I ever would from public schooling. The main reason? Because I like what I'm learning. I remember it, because I find it interesting. The more interesting the subject is, the more likely it'll stick with me.

When I lived in Indiana, I was surrounded with mainly kids

who'd been public schooled their whole lives, and hadn't even heard of "homeschooling." My two brothers were too young to be quite "desperate" for friends yet, and my older sister spent a lot of her time traveling to other states to stay with the friends she had.

I wanted friends too, ones who I could see on the weekdays, and ones who didn't only want to talk about their classmates, classes, and teachers. The one homeschooled friend I actually had, had such an organized home-learning schedule and such a strict curriculum, I felt I never got to see her. Therefore, I was the one piece of funky in a world of normals.

Now that I've moved to Oregon I've found a huge homeschooling community. Teen groups, study groups, and best of all, friends. I created my own group known as the SG1 and every one of them is either homeschooled or unschooled. They have taught me lots of things, but one of the ones I found most impressive was that I didn't feel stupid anymore when I asked questions. Where I used to live, if I asked someone a question, they'd usually reply in such a condescending way I felt foolish for asking. They made me feel I was under-educated because there were areas that I didn't meet the Public School standards of education. My new friends, my homeschooled friends, are all at such different levels in so many different areas, that I fit right into that funkiness.

At 17, I won't lie and say I've never been curious about public school. I even once considered "shadowing" someone for a day or two when I still lived in Indiana. I decided against it for two reasons: The first is that I would miss my family. Like most families, when we're home, we spread out, dispersed to our separate places of enjoyment. My dad goes to the garage, my brothers sit at their computer or Wii, my mom begins working upstairs and I go to my room to do my own writing. Despite this, we come together for meals. Whether we go out or stay home, our meals are spent laughing and joking. In the evenings, we gather to watch a movie, or turn on the latest episode of our favorite TV series. These two times are often where most of our homeschooling conversations come up. Just as often, they are unplanned. The idea of going to school, and substituting my meals with them for sitting in a cafeteria, and my evenings of gathering on our couch for sitting in my room with mountains of homework certainly doesn't appeal to me. The other reason? Like most of my friends, I'm not crazy about getting up early!

I try not to be stereotypical about public schooling, but I've been down that road so many times, in so many different ways, I find it hard not to be. I've befriended public schoolers, I've babysat for them and I've even dated them, and never has the experience turned out well. I've lost several friends who were homeschoolers for most their lives, and then went to public school, whether it was by their decision, or their parents'. They simply change too much. I try to be an open-minded person, but my experience has hardened me. I've tried hanging with a public schooled group of teens, and found myself treated an outsider. I've attempted to attend public schooled camps, such as Girl Scout camp, and found myself insulted daily and offended often, and have even been physically assaulted.

In homeschooling ages blend together. In public schools as well as most private schools, the ages are separated from the time they arrive until the time they leave. When they do have the chance to mix, the idea is already in their heads that they aren't supposed to mingle with other "grades." In homeschooling, there is almost none of that. I lead a group called the Walking Legends. They are a group of homeschoolers ranging between 11 and 19 years old who explore different parts of Portland's wonders together. The ages mingle all the time, no matter where we go. They talk, they laugh and joke, and they find things in common, regardless of the difference in age.

My parents have made a lot of good decisions in my life. Homeschooling is one of the best. Besides the fact that I believe homeschooling brings better and easier education to the "student," I also think that it brings the family together. Getting out of the "norm" of public schooling and into "home learning" is so very worth it in my eyes. Today, I am surrounded by a lot of funkiness—and guess what? It's all normal.

~ Nicole

When I was six years old, my parents decided to pull me out of public school. The reasons are many, but suffice it to say the school was not interested in changing their educational philosophies to fit the needs of each individual child: instead, they prefer a method our family likens to "one size fits all."

At the age of 6, which would be first grade, I was already reading fluently. Often times I would read from *National Geographic* or *Reader's Digest* magazines laying around the house. In first grade, they began to teach us phonics. As you can imagine it is not much help to try and teach a reader how to read. Sort of like giving driving lessons to Mario Andretti. Because I was bored, learning what I already knew, the wheels were set in motion to diagnose me with Attention Deficit Disorder. My parents were not thrilled, so at the end of my first grade year, they decided to remove me from the public school system and opt for a do-it-yourself approach. My mother told me, "You never have to go back to public school again." I cried from relief.

One of the things which amazed me the most was not needing permission to use the bathroom. In school, you must raise your hand to ask, and then if you take "too long" (as happened to me more than once) the teacher walks right into the stall you are using to be sure you're not up to anything.

After beginning homeschooling I noticed a few things which I could not articulate at the time. Mainly I no longer felt like a suspect. As with the aforementioned bathroom inspections, I always felt like they were just waiting for me to do something wrong. With some perspective on the issue, I now realize where the average teacher is coming from. With 30 kids to look after, many of whom are unruly and/or hyperactive, a person could learn to become pessimistic and expect the worst. But is this really the environment a child should grow up in?

At home I was treated to a caring family environment without the educational and peer pressures associated with school. Instead of being harassed by people I didn't like and being jabbed with pencils, instead of waiting to go out on the playground because I wasn't a Self Manager, I was allowed freedom. My mother was the primary teacher for many years because my father worked a very full week. He usually didn't come home before 6 o'clock on week-nights, and when I was younger he worked the occasional Saturday. This left me, my mother and my sister, six years younger than I, in my "classroom." As I was soon to discover, my classroom was much larger than most.

For several years my "curriculum" was comprised mostly of trips to the library where we were allowed to check out as many books as we could carry. Trips to the grocery store, where we learned comparative shopping. The Discovery, Learning and History channels on TV. The kitchen table, where we learned about finances, the importance of paying bills on time and how to balance a checkbook. We even learned basic algebra together—my sister and I weren't the only ones that were learning either.

I feel that this time spent with my family doing not only independent academic research and learning real-world skills gave me a head start on life. Where public school attempts to specifically teach you abilities, like problem solving and research skills, homeschooling allowed my sister and myself to learn them by doing. By being allowed to pursue what we wanted when we wanted, we learned how to use valuable tools like the library. There was no set beginning and end time. If we were tired of reading about World War II, we could return the book and check out a new one on the space program.

We also purchased a fair selection of books from the second-hand store near our house. As my mother always told us, "Books are an investment, not an expense."

It remained true even when money was very tight.

When I left school, I did not enjoy reading, math or writing. After years of independent study, after looking at hundreds of *National Geographic* maps and charts underneath the plastic cover on the dinner table. And free access to all the arts, crafts and writing materials I could ever use, I am now an aspiring author attending and paying for my own college. I feel that time with adults who have been through life, instead of with people my age who can only hazard a guess from what they've seen on television has given me a much more mature view on the world.

I make this claim having been to junior and high-school for band and choir. My sister and I have both been completely able to go to school if we wanted to. In junior high I was reintroduced not only to the very same unsure guesses at what the world is about, but the same ignorant and intolerant attitudes, now much more established in these kids' minds. In high school I saw the swirling vortex that either sucks you in, or throws you back out. Either a person is popular, or they think for themselves and are often ostracized. Groups of individual thinkers misguided each other into drugs or alcohol. Anyone who's been there knows what I'm talking about.

Because I had the time to reflect on what kind of person I wanted to be, because I was not forced to associate with anyone I didn't want to be around, I matured into the person most highschoolers are struggling to become, well before entering school. While there, I felt a little like the odd man out—different from the others—but not in a bad way. I have never tried drugs or alcohol. I was not concerned when someone informed me my clothes were uncool. Their thoughts on the matter did not affect me. While others would spend time bashing their parents and complaining about them, I had nothing to add. My family was still close, even to a 14 year old. I could hug my parents in sight of everyone and not care. So in addition to educational freedom and family solidarity, I feel I gained a maturity that many people never really gain.

When we began to homeschool employees of various stores would always ask "No school today?" if we went shopping during school hours. We were regarded as an oddity. Thirteen years later it's quite common to see other homeschoolers. Often times they're easy to spot. The parents and children are speaking to each other as equals. The children are respectful and see absolutely nothing wrong with enjoying time around their parents.

For certain, the number of us has grown dramatically from when we began back in 1990s. Thousands and thousands of people, each with a unique reason, whether it's a lack of satisfaction with the system or simply a parent's desire to remain active in their child's education, whether the child has special needs or the family wants their children to embrace a religious way of thinking, homeschooling has something to offer anyone who wants to try it. ~ Matt

There's a Buddhist philosophy that states that life is based upon great change. Without change and evolution, nothing can ever reach its true potential. School made me tunnel-visioned, and deciding to leave it knocked the tunnel down. It was the biggest and most positive change I've ever made, and it continues to ripple outward into the tiniest crevices, making everything about my life wide open and wonderful.

There was never anything wrong with traditional school: in fact, I rather fancied it. Ambition was always my thing, so I strove for pitch-perfect grades and made it my driving force. At age 13, I was acing classes and clamoring around the city with my bundle of grade-greedy girlfriends and feeling pretty on top of my game. It was at this pinnacle of my preteen sassiness that my mother confronted me: we were moving. The idea of a school transfer was frustrating—crushing even—and a new city, even worse. We fought. And fought. And finally, searched for compromise.

That compromise was homeschooling. A temporary change, my mother assured me, and one we would have plenty of control over. It would be structured. I could even get ahead of the game and earn extra credits. I consented reluctantly.

After I left public school, the walls and boundaries I had put up began to blur and melt down softly. A year was no longer nine months of work and a summer. A project was no longer about the notes I took, or the mark I got on it when it was done. Because Mom had trust in my own self-motivation, the structure we talked about was only loosely put together, and soon I was floating about in this strange new freedom. It made me wide-eyed and curious. I found writing was pleasurable—not grunt work, and discovered poetry and playwriting. I found theatre didn't need to be done in an "acting class;" I could go out and volunteer for a company all on my own. I saw that one's world did not need to be so segmented, scheduled, and measured. It could move about freely like water, instead of wood.

For me, transitions and changes have become a welcome and wonderful part of living. Without this great change, I probably wouldn't know or care about Buddhism (let alone philosophies contained within it) unless, of course, it was included in some special assignment. To my mother and to homeschooling, I owe my outlook on life and what learning should be—a study in freedom and personal evolution.

-Maggie

I am a former public schooler and adult unschooler, and I am strongly against compulsory schooling. I believe that people all learn in different ways and at different speeds. The problem with forced compulsory schooling is that very rarely are these differences taken into consideration.

I hardly remember my life before I was in a school of some kind. I started preschool part time when I was three years old, and only left schooling two months ago – 16 years after starting. Most of my time in school (aside from preschool, a year of college, and a dual enrollment between my high school and a community college) was spent within public schools in suburban, upper middle class Washington.

I didn't like school. I hated it most of the time I went. I resented being forced there, and being forced to do work with a purpose I didn't understand. I had some good years. Sixth grade, for instance, was a blast. I had great classmates and a really cool teacher. I actually liked being there a lot of the time. Too bad this was the exception, and not the norm.

In studying alternative education and the arguments against compulsory schooling, I've come to see many reasons to dislike school that didn't even bother me as a student. I didn't mind the social culture at my schools. People were, on the whole, pretty cool. There were cliques, but nothing as bad as movies portray. I always had a good group of friends (though, not always the same friends every year). If I bothered to study and complete my homework on time, I received good grades. I didn't struggle with comprehension. I was active in various school groups from elementary school onward. I wasn't a "problem student."

Internally, though, I had a really hard time continuously being forced to go to a place I didn't want to. Why was I spending six hours a day in various classrooms, listening to teachers ramble on as I tried not to fall asleep? Why did I have pages and pages of homework to do once the school day was done? Why were teachers annoyed if I chose to work by myself instead of in a team, or if I chose to work in a team instead of by myself? Why were people so competitive about grades? Why did people place so much of their self-worth into what grade they got? Why were we given "progress reports" to bring home to our parents for a signature on our grade? How was that one letter supposed to encompass all we thought, felt, and learned in a class? Why were we being taught how to pass tests, instead of how to love subjects? Why did we have to ask permission to use the restroom? Why did we only have five minutes to get from class to class, or else face a detention? Why were we segregated by age? Why were we required to take certain subjects and not encouraged to study others? Why were we told that our futures depended on our "success" in this system? Why did no one else seem to notice a problem with any of this?

I discovered alternative schooling when I was a frustrated, depressed ninth grade honors student. I had been fooling around online, procrastinating on homework and googling phrases like "school is boring" when I discovered my first website advocating alternative education. From there, I kept researching and learning about these new ideas. I discovered authors John Taylor Gatto, Grace Llewellyn, and John Holt. I discovered that I was not the only student who could get by in school, not have disciplinary problems, but also definitely not like being there. I felt like my feelings were finally validated. I also discovered unschooling, the style of education that I feel my personal beliefs fit most closely with. And with the discovery of unschooling came the discovery of Not Back To School Camp (NBTSC), a camp for unschooled teenagers.

I wanted to try full-time unschooling. I tried to explain it to my parents, but they didn't go along with the idea. In the end, it was more important for me to finish school, however resentfully, than possibly forever ruin my relationship with them. And to my surprise and happiness, after much discussion, they allowed me the opportunity to attend NBTSC. I was seventeen, and it was the summer before my senior year of high school.

Basically, Not Back To School Camp changed my life, in dramatic and positive ways. I learned how to hug, to open up more to people, to love others unconditionally. I also was socializing for the first time with homeschoolers and unschoolers, not just public schoolers.

In public school, many people have preconceived ideas of what home schoolers are like. And even in the extremely nonjudgmental atmosphere of NBTSC, I noticed people there had prejudices of what public schoolers were like. I experienced times where I felt divided between both these very different cultures and I *like* the people in both cultures. That's one thing I feel very strongly about. People in public school, people who homeschool, and people who unschool can all be wonderful. I've had the pleasure to meet people who fit into all these categories. I do identify as an (ex) public schooler *and* an unschooler. I don't believe a person has to not attend school growing up to be an unschooler. I feel I'm unschooling myself now, pursuing my own hobbies and interests when I'm not at work (as well as working at jobs that allow me to learn new skills and information I'm interested in knowing). I also want to become involved in advocacy for alternative education. I think the public school format can, and does, work for some people. It just does not work for everyone, and I think it's about time people quit pretending that it should. Compulsory schooling is flawed, for it is *compulsory*. People go to school because they are forced, not because they choose to be there. If people who didn't want to be there were free to pursue other interests, or other styles of school, and the people who want to be there were the only ones there, it seems to me that everyone would have an easier time learning.

I don't regret not trying harder to get out of public school. I definitely didn't like the experience, and plan to unschool my own children if I have any someday, but I'm glad for what I learned from the experience. I think it's really beneficial that I got to experience what public school was like. I know firsthand what doesn't work about it, or at least, what didn't work in the schools I attended. I know what

I'd like to see changed. I know what I'd like to educate people about, so that maybe more will be done to make the changes that are necessary in order for youth to grow up more healthy, happy, and satisfied with their lives.

~ Emily

Voices of Experience

Traveling, Homeschooling and Learning to Relax (Jasmine's story, part 1, written in 2001)

I remember my tee shirt being stuck to my back with dense Las Vegas sweat as I sat on my jam-packed maroon bag on the floor of the Greyhound bus station. The woman to my left kept asking me if I wanted to come and play the slot machines with her before the bus came. The woman to my right was making her hot dog say, "No, please don't eat me!" before shoving it in her mouth. And I still had two hours left to wait.

I love traveling.

It was the last day of September, and I'd already been gone for a little over a month. I'd left my home in northern Indiana, spent the night at a friend's house in Minnesota, driven the rest of the way out to Oregon, spending the night in various hotels along the way; I'd already stayed in three hotels in Eugene, Oregon, two friend's houses, and had been to two weeks of camp. I'd taken a road trip down to Southern California with another friend and stayed there for a week and then early that morning, I had taken a Greyhound bus out of Los Angeles to finally come to this resting point—mid-afternoon in Las Vegas, sitting on the gritty ground in a heat wave listening to some crazy woman make her hot dog screech in pain.

And I still had almost three months left.

Here in Las Vegas, I was searching for something to do. Finally, I pulled out my road atlas and began paging through it, all the dog-eared pages, all the little notes along the margins. Soon, I was circling all the places I'd been to on a list on the contents page. Much to the amazement of the talking-hot-dog lady, it was over half of the country.

"Where do you get all the time?" She asked in admiration, her hot dog momentarily silent. "You know, with school and all?" I just grinned and kept circling.

After my layover in Las Vegas, I spent five weeks in Colorado with a most wonderful boy, then two and a half weeks in Minnesota working at a Christmas tree farm, then two more weeks in Colorado, before driving out to my new home in Oregon. I was gone for four months. In some ways, it seemed like forever. At the same time, it didn't come close to quelling my obsession with traveling. Now, after being home only a month, I'm already pining to leave again. Time to mark another state off the list, time to get some more ticket stubs for my wall collage, time to experience somewhere new.

I've been traveling sporadically since I was 12—various summer camps, train rides, flights, road trips, and more often than anything else, Greyhound Lines Incorporated excursions. Now, five years later, I have an entire wall collage of ticket stubs, itineraries, baggage claims, and bus schedules. I have another wall collage full of photographs of all the places I've been, the people I've met, the things I've seen, and each object is a piece of evidence that I am living "out of the box."

As a lifetime homeschooler, it has become a somewhat necessary part of my life to explain things (like where I get all my time) to what seems like everyone. The amount of ignorance so many people think I have is nothing compared to the ignorance people have about homeschooling. The majority of people blindly accept the stereotypes—that all of us homeschoolers are religious, that we are stuck all day doing textbook work, that we are sadly removed from all possibilities of socialization. Sometimes, these ideas are so deeply ingrained in people's minds that even after I explain thoroughly the actual truths about my education style, they still retain their beliefs. And people call me stubborn!

A huge discrepancy in the information that most people have is that we are going to miss out… not to mention fall behind with our grades, end up friendless and lonely all through our adolescence, be unable to attend college later in life, etc. On the bad days, it seems like simply everybody is loaded with misconceptions like these. I can't believe sometimes where these ideas originated. While most children are removed from the "real world," I was thrown headfirst in the middle of it, innocent and blinking with wide eyes, full of the drive to learn hands-on—not post-graduation—but right from birth. What's the point of waiting, of allowing my mind to be shaped and molded to the whims of another? Shouldn't it really be my own choice how my mind evolves? There is no better way to reach new and fascinating ideas than through boredom, and although school gives plenty of that, kids are left with no drive to learn outside of school. After years of being force fed knowledge that they will never use by some person somewhere who deemed that it was part of the appropriate curriculum for a grade, they are burnt out.

There are days when it's easy to get angry. These are the days when people seem to be constantly at your throat about your educational decision, leaving you thinking that there isn't a single open-minded person left on the whole planet. We homeschoolers get crazy, completely uninformed questions like, "Are you still smart?" "Don't you miss seeing other kids?" "What's two plus two?" and my personal favorite, "How will you ever learn to answer the phone?" At times, it just takes too much energy to sit and explain that OF COURSE I'm still smart; I see a more diverse group of people than they ever did. Can't you ask me a **real** question (and what does not being in school have to do with learning how to answer the phone)? But at the end of the day, when I can spend my evening doing anything but homework, when I am halfway across the country from home, when I am just sitting on my bed thinking, I have never once regretted the way in which I learn.

It is incredible the options and new opportunities homeschooling or unschooling can present. But can't people just stop worrying? When I sit down and attempt to explain things, I am hit with the same series of questions, each one like a slap of ignorance across my face. Instead of weighing the advantages and disadvantages, there are only all the worries, all the assumptions, all the misconceptions people refuse to relinquish. There are times when I've sat down and gone over each and every detail, and the conclusion is always to stop worrying. Removing yourself from school is the easiest way to pull out all the stops. My lack of textbook learning will never do anything to obstruct my going to college or having a busy social life. I have the resourcefulness and wherewithal to pursue the exact areas of study I find exciting and to begin working toward my desired occupation. While I watch dozens of school buses haul kids away, I am tying my shoes to go to work that earns me the paychecks that I save up to buy tickets to go and explore other states. Everything I do is building on my life experience—experience that I am racking up in the hours that all the other kids my age are sitting in neat rows of desks, studying things they'll forget as soon as the test is over. Kids look gray colored as they pass by me, while I feel like brilliant technicolor.

In not going to school, a few doors have been closed. I will not go to a school prom. I will not play on a school sports team. I will miss out on having a huge graduation ceremony with a cap and gown. But yet, in closing these few doors, I have simultaneously thrown open dozens more. Not being in school, I have been given the opportunity to have many different part-time jobs, meet people of all ages and from all over the country, not to mention the world, gone to over half of the states and fallen in love with writing and theatre. I've been forced to build my own education, and in doing so, found a love for learning. I have found heroes and poets; I've encountered opposition and discovered ways to always get around someone telling me "no." I am living proof that there is hope in the world. I've read hundreds of books, filled dozens of notebooks, and taken insane amounts of photographs. I have time to sit and think about the world, to consider ways to change it, how things might be some day, and at the same time, play with a barrel of monkeys and make magazine clipping collages. I know where my priorities are.

The best available advice is relax. When out in the midst of freedom, everything is so much easier. There is an added level of excitement; there is the newfound pursuit of something new everyday and the urge to absorb everything. It is a wide-eyed, hands on approach to poetry, traveling, lights, and words. It is like a present at the foot of your bed every morning when you awake, a box filled with ideas that thrill, concepts that amaze, opportunities that ignite something within. Just imagine having your entire life to yourself. Imagine your eyes opening one morning and realizing that it isn't just an eternal summer vacation, it is eternal freedom. Never once have I been forced to miss out on anything by not going to school, because in being in control of myself, I've been handed the world.

Loud Music Cures Everything
(Jasmine's Story, part 2, written in 2007)

"What we don't understand we can make mean anything."

Chuck Palahniuk wrote that in his book *Diary*, and that's what I was thinking about instead of out trying to save the world like usual as youth outreach worker. I was eating chocolate bars from a big bag and sitting on a red vinyl couch that squeaked every time I moved my legs. That's what I was thinking about instead of the meeting that I was supposed to be participating in, except that in a flurry of motion and vague decisions, half of the staff had left to search someone's bags for a gun he may or may not have on him and the other half to do an impromptu intervention on a teen mother who was just seen beating her toddler with a belt. A few of us stayed behind, not wanting to overcrowd either situation.

As I looked out the window at the first really heavy downpour of the season, I realized that if I was someone else, this moment might be really intense. If I was someone else, I might nervous, overwhelmed or flustered. If I was someone else reading this, I might think that I seem really cold and jaded. But mostly I'm just eating chocolate and thinking of a quote from a book I read on a road trip last summer. This day is not particularly awful; my brain is comparing it to the stabbing and the stroke and the overdose and the kid that threatened to jump off the top of our building and the people that leave town and just never come back and in my warped and distanced brain, this moment just doesn't quite compare. I'm paid to be able to handle these days. My paychecks are direct rewards for being able to stay calm in life or death situations and to be unconditionally compassionate to people that always need compassion but don't always want it. The fact is—I'm stressed out. The fact is—homeless drug-addicted youth lead very drama-filled lives and now I'm a part of it too.

"What we don't understand we can make mean anything." That's why a man in a sharp suit with a briefcase can walk by a group of homeless kids asking for spare change on a street corner and can make it mean that they are lazy bums that just need to go get jobs.

That's why when someone looks at these amazing kids I know with the track marks on their arms and their teeth rotting out of their heads, they can make it all mean that they are a bunch of lost causes to just walk by and ignore.

That's why when an adult looks at a kid, any kid, anywhere, they can make it mean that they deserve to act like they are smarter and better.

That's why when I walk into a business with a stack of freshly printed resumes, someone can look at me with my tattoos and my piercings and my neon orange hair and make it mean that I will be an inappropriate, unprofessional, untrustworthy liability and won't even take my job application.

It's also why now, when I am 23 years old, someone like my boss can look at my homeschooled high school diploma and make that piece of paper mean that I am not eligible for a 50 cent raise for my job; that I am already doing just fine.

And it's all because what we don't understand, we can make mean anything. I use this to my advantage as often as possible, because I believe you should milk every opportunity for all it's worth. Bleed every option dry. Leave the brittle bones of every potential adventure already investigated and discarded behind to bleach in the sun. Let the vultures come. I don't care. I've already moved down the highway, already become a new person, already evolved.

But what we don't understand, we can make mean anything, which is why I decided at that moment—while half my meeting curbs child abuse and the other half erases the possibility of fatal violence in the near future—that it all meant that I've come pretty far.

I've grown up and figured a lot of stuff out. Every moment you're alive, you're learning something, absorbing things, your brain is constantly inhaling, if you want an absurd analogy. The thing is, some of that stuff you learn isn't very good for you: high fructose corn syrup thoughts, hydrogenated oil opinions and tar-colored facts that aren't facts at all. They're all in a greasy disguise. This is a round about way of saying that I'm pretty pleased with my decision to throw out the guidelines of the low-calorie, low-flavor diet that public school might have assigned to my brain and go for my own disgustingly rich regimen. I fully intend on feeding my brain a big chunk of chocolate cake everyday for as long as I can get away with it.

It has been a long time since I carried that official label of "lifetime unschooler" around as a big part of my identity. I ponder what it is like being an adult that never went to school. It's honestly easier said than done. How am I supposed to know what its like to be an adult who DID go? Part of me would like to say that I am a mature, independent, free thinking and successful girl because I was given the spectacular chance to grow up without stifling structure and ugly conformity.

At the same time, I'd also like to say that I'm a reasonably clever orange-haired artist type of girl who is stubborn and fights for all that is good and right and especially exciting in the world and believes herself and her own gut above all else. I would like to say that I would be this odd and eclectic and brash person regardless of the role that school ended up taking in my life. But I can't know. Those cards have already been played and now I'm playing a different game entirely and concentrating on staying a high roller. So I'm not sure how to compare my experience to anyone else's. I don't know how my life could have been.

   The purest thing I can think of is that I was partly given—but mostly demanded—the right to fill my brain with whatever I wanted it filled with, which is why you won't find a list of state capitals or any algebra in there. I jam packed the available space with a lot of memories of insane Greyhound bus trips and all of the lyrics to "Hey Jude." I decided to ignore all the information in typical history textbooks and traded it in for the truth about Christopher Columbus and the ugly drunken prose of Charles Bukowski. I did away with learning how white man conquers everything he touches and read about genocide in South Africa instead. I gave away grammar and sentence structure and learned how to cut up my clothes and reinvent them. I said no thank you to the shallow jungle of the cafeteria for the savage existence of Hunter S. Thompson. I never learned anything about Home Ec. I just decided to get a full time job or two instead. What we don't understand, we can make mean anything.

   Since I wrote "Traveling, Homeschooling and Trying to Relax," a lot has happened in my life. I moved to Portland with my first boyfriend. We both got jobs at an ice cream shop. My boss and I fought on the issues of sexism and I left before getting fired. Next, I got a job at a bakery in the mall's food court and wrote many angst filled poems about my time being worth more than minimum wage. Next, I managed a hot-tub-by-the-hour place, not realizing it would include a meth-addicted boss and calling 911 on overdosing prostitutes. I worked at a porn store and met many strippers, got my lip pierced and cleaned up things I would rather forget. I learned to chase down shoplifters, wear an awful uniform and then applied for a job in social work. I got it!

   Now, my brain is filled with images of abuse and addiction and madness. I listen to bands like "The Good Life," "Bright Eyes" and "Okkervil River" very loud in a dark apartment to cleanse the wounds of the day. My stupid heart shrivels up and is reborn every morning, slightly stronger. I met boys who seemed sweet and turned sour and then, somewhere along the line, I got married and stayed that way. I discover the manic seizure of my brain the first time I saw art by Ralph Steadman. I read *What is the What* by Dave Eggers and I dream of holding hands with every *Lost Boy* in Sudan. I got other jobs, a dog, a bike.

I make friends with bartenders, junkies, painters, social activists and gutter punks. I keep my hair dyed varying shades of ridiculous. Elliott Smith died and I immediately felt very old. George Bush got re-elected and my city exploded with unbearable rage and venom and lay across the highways and we mess with Iraq anyway.

My sense of purpose grows smaller and larger depending on the weather and what books I've read lately. I read books by Jonathon Safran Foer and it gets bigger. I read books about torture in South African prisons and I lose hope. I became intensely fascinated by the counter culture and the drug culture waves of the 70's and I feel like a girl anachronism. I went to many concerts and stand at the front and forget work and life and whatever else is out there and remain constantly amazed by the way your heart can adapt to beat in time with a really good base line if it's loud enough. It's a fact: Loud Music Cures Everything. If you turn certain songs up loud enough, it's certainly better than the drugs I watch all the street youth take. All you need is that rising sound. Read about it in *Fear and Loathing in Las Vegas*. I highly suggest it.

What we don't understand we can make mean anything. I thought about it all through that meeting, while I rode my bike home, while sitting in my apartment and at the pub down the street.

There are things I know I don't know. I don't understand how to earn enough money to buy a house, how to say no to picking up extra shifts or how to keep my apartment as clean as I'd like to. This simply means I've got a lot left to learn.

On the other hand, I do understand how to get and keep a job, how to maintain a healthy relationship, how to treat my friends and how I deserve to treated, which means I've learned a lot.

I also understand how to advocate for myself, which is why in the long run I ended up getting that 50 cent raise. I won! What we don't understand we can make mean anything, which is comforting because I think that this means I win all the time.

Chapter 7

The What Ifs and What Abouts?

"We must not allow other people's limited perceptions to define us."

~ Virginia Satir
author and psychotherapist
specializing in family therapy

There is little within the realm of parenting that doesn't cause moments of self-doubt, and homeschooling is certainly no exception to the rule. There will be moments where even the most veteran parent will stop and wonder if he/she is doing the right thing, responding the right way, providing the right material, etc. This simply means that your children and their education is important to you and you want to make sure you are doing the best job you possibly can. This doesn't imply perfection; none of us can reach that level (although there are moments we feel mighty brilliant!) and shouldn't attempt to try. Don't let yourself fall into the trap of comparison either. Just because the homeschooling family down the block has made a life size rocket in their back yard which they are planning to fly to Mars when the weather improves, or the other homeschoolers around the corner have children who have each invented something that recently sold a billion copies, it doesn't indicate that you are doing a bad job because you haven't done the same. It just means that you are doing different things. Not all homeschooled children go on to become rock stars, millionaires, best selling authors or Nobel Prize winners; instead the kids just tend to be happy, educated, intelligent and fulfilled—not a bad goal to aspire to at all.

This chapter is all about those questions that pop up in your head in the middle of the night when you are supposed to be sleeping. That "what if this happens?" or "what about this situation?" question can often create a healthy case of insomnia for us parental units. Just as with any parenting question, there are answers that will fit you and your children and ones that won't. Hopefully, these suggestions and ideas will, at last, give you something to think about and new options to consider.

What if my child doesn't have any friends?

We all want our children to have friends. It's easy to be parent and playmate when your children are still small, but the older they get, the more they will yearn for others closer to their age to relate to. For some, making friends just seems easier than for others, whether in public school or homeschool. Shy children, or those who just appear to be loners, can be more challenging than the outgoing, talking-a-mile-a-minute kind of kid. Your location will make a big difference too; obviously, larger cities are going to have more opportunities than smaller ones. Some of the places you can find peers for your kids include 4-H clubs, Girl Scouts, Boy Scouts, church groups, YM/YWCAs, sports groups and naturally, homeschool groups. Enroll your child in local classes, workshops and volunteer organizations. Each one opens up the chance to meet new people and perhaps make more friends in the process.

Summer camps are also a great way for kids to meet others. Depending on your philosophy and your available choices, you may want to choose an all homeschooling camp. My four kids have gone to camp since they were old enough to not be homesick anymore. My oldest went to Girl Scout camp and then became a counselor there. Not Back to School Camp was a turning point in her life. My next daughter has been to more camps than I can count, as both a camper and a "gear," a dishwasher who then attends for free. She has been able to go by doing a number of work-trades, allowing her more chances to go and also teaching a great deal about responsibility. Not Back to School camp is only one of her choices each summer, but it is always her favorite. Both girls came home with lists of new friends from all over the country; some they still get to see in person, while others became online friends and travel hosts.

As my sons mature, their camp time has arrived. The third one has gone to Not Back to School Camp as well and has met some great people there. The fourth one is still too young but is counting the days.

Remember too that homeschoolers can often make friends in places you might not have thought of. Because they have not been put in school and segregated by age and grade level, they commonly do not carry the concept that you can only be buddies with people your own age. These children are frequently as able to make friends with a child three or four years younger or with an adult 20 years older. They might love playing with a toddler who idolizes them or enjoy the conversations and games they play with people at a local nursing home.

If you live in a remote area, it's going to be harder to find others to talk to, play with and just hang out with. Choices here might have to incorporate email and instant messaging buddies, pen pals and some long distance trips to and from friends' houses.

Also, consider hosting regular (weekly, monthly) events at your house or other facility that brings homeschoolers to you. You might organize a teen group, a play date, a potluck dinner—whatever you feel like handling. By bringing families to you, your children have the chance to meet other kids—and you have the chance to hang and connect with other parents. For me, an added bonus is it makes me clean the house when otherwise I would just let another dust layer make itself at home.

If your child is struggling to meet kids, don't let yourself fall into the trap of thinking that putting him into public school will solve the entire issue. He may have just as much trouble there, if not more, or he may make the kind of friends that you would never have wanted him to.

Some children have a very strong drive for friends, and for those children you will need to seek out new opportunities. Some want to know a lot of children on a lighter level; others crave close relationships with just one or two people. Other children enjoy either alone time or have a sibling that fills a good portion of the need for friends. (Yes, my friend, it is possible for siblings to also be friends!)

The friendship situation changes for each family, depending on location, personality and other factors. Rest assured, however, it is a very, very rare child that doesn't have any friends at all.

What if we have to move?

The most important thing to investigate, if you are going to move to another state, is what the homeschooling laws are there. If they are more lenient, smile and be grateful. If they are stricter, start talking to other homeschoolers in that area and see what they have to say. Reading the law alone is not enough; check to see how well or often it is actually enforced, what loopholes exist, etc. Also consider this: most likely the state you are moving to will not know of your existence (I speak from experience here, having moved six years ago from Indiana to Oregon), so how much you want to comply is up to you.

Go on the Internet or check with homeschooling magazines and find out where the support groups are in the area where you are moving. Join their chat rooms or special interest groups and start asking important questions. What are the libraries like there? What is the overall homeschooling environment? What activities are available? What are some of the best ways to get connected with others? When and where do support groups meet? If you move to a new area with this information, it will make the transition easier for everyone. You will have the information you need and your kids will have a head start on meeting new friends and finding new opportunities.

When we moved here, I had done a lot of footwork ahead of time. I had talked to families, joined a support group and announced our arrival. On the day we pulled into our new driveway with the moving truck, four families were waiting there. They spent three hours helping us unload the truck, carry in boxes, unpack and set up. They had never met us before—and to this day, we still are not sure who was here that day. However, the kindness of that gesture assured our entire family that we had made the right decision in coming to this city.

What if my child wants to go to school?

The answer to this depends greatly on the age and experience of the child. Small children may want to go to kindergarten because they hear so much hype about it on television commercials, preschool, friends' houses and other places. Young ones often have a very idealistic picture of what school is like—lots of time to play, new toys, tons of other kids ALL of whom will be new best friends—they aren't aware of all the downsides that come with school. Taking time to discuss this with your young child will help; just knowing you have to have permission to go to the bathroom may be enough to change their minds.

Older children, on the other hand, may feel pressured to go to public school by friends or by all the promo each fall for back to school supplies, new clothes, etc. I remember one mother I met at a book signing. She was almost in tears and said her six-year-old wanted to go to school. The little one was with her, so I asked her what it was about school that she liked. Her big brown eyes looked up at me and she said, "I want the glittery folders and pencils my friend got."

Problem solved, Mom. Just take her to the store and get her some glittery folders of her own.

The first step to addressing this situation is pinpointing what it is your child really wants. It is rarely gong to be school itself but new clothes, new friends, the excitement of the new year, the chance to be in band or on the baseball team and so on. If you can figure out what they are truly searching for, then you can begin to address it. If they are lured by "Back to School" supplies, taken them to the store and let them pick out what they like. Even if they use them for non-educational related purposes (are there any truly non-educational related purposes?), what is the harm? If it's new clothes they are wishing for, budget them in if possible.

If the main reason your children want to go to school is curiosity (and it often is), consider having them shadow another student at school for a day or two. Pick a neighbor child, friend, or cousin whom your child can follow around to classes and see what different aspects of school are like. (You will need to check in with your local school system first to make sure this is allowed.) Be prepared for a variety of responses. One woman who allowed her 15-year-old to shadow a friend at the local junior high said she spent most of her day with fingers crossed that her daughter wouldn't like it. She was amazingly relieved when her teen walked through the front door, plopped down on the couch and exclaimed that she had never seen a group of people waste that much time in her entire life. She was shocked at the amount of busy work involved in a normal school day and couldn't believe anyone would want to spend their days in such a regimented place.

Conversely, if your child spends a few days in school and seems to love it, you are faced with two possible options. First, you can let him enroll. Second, you can refuse. If you choose option one, make sure you talk carefully and at length first about your concerns and let him know that this is a temporary situation—he can always come back home. Please don't take the attitude of "If I enroll you, mister, than you are in for the whole year. Don't come and tell me you have changed your mind." This simply is not fair. How many times, as adults, have we made decisions that we immediately regretted? We're talking about a child here. Give him the freedom to make a decision and then, if he finds it was the wrong one, the freedom to change his mind.

Consider talking to the school and see if you can enroll your child part time as a compromise. This would be a slower introduction to the public school world.

If you choose not to enroll him despite his desire, be up front about your reasons why and be willing to listen to his thoughts and ideas respectfully and openly. Younger children will most likely cope better than older ones who also don't want you picking out their socks anymore, let alone telling them where they can and cannot go to school. It can be a difficult time and if your child keeps insisting month after month, be prepared to reconsider your decision.

What if my child never learns to read?

When I first wrote the answer to this question, I had a 17 year old who had essentially taught herself to read at six and the others were ten, seven and four, so I was not particularly concerned about the issue yet. Since then, I have seen such incredible diversity in how my kids learned to read that I was amazed. My second child learned at 12; my third at six (in less than 24 hours!) and my fourth at almost 14. Today, all of them read above grade level and often switch books with one another.

Worrying about if your child will read is one of those questions that strikes you at 3 a.m. when you are on your way back to bed from a pee break. It is just part of the "what if" mindset that we parents can get ourselves into sometimes. Of course your child will learn to read if you follow a few basic steps: (1) Read to her often; (2) Have all different kinds of books readily available and accessible and (3) Read yourself so you set a good role model. (It's hard to sell how wonderful reading is if you never do it yourself!)

Will your child start to read by age six? Perhaps. . . perhaps not. What does it matter? Just because school has trained us to think that children must read at six years old doesn't mean it is remotely true. Did your child take his first step on the day he turned one year old? Or was it at nine months? Or 15 months? Did that mean he was gifted—or challenged? No! It just meant that he did it when *he was ready*. The same thing goes for reading, writing, math, or any other subject at hand. Children do things, if they are allowed, when they are ready. It might be before or after *you* are ready, but children need to go by their own timetable, not yours.

Homeschooling will not necessarily guarantee that your child will be a voracious reader (or so I've heard . . . all of mine are voracious readers, but I am sure there are others who are not), but not having it forced on him when he isn't ready, as happens every single day in public school, will certainly increase his chances. Allowing your child to learn to do things at his own pace and style isn't always easy; your experience keeps telling you that a child of "x" years old *must* know how to do "y." It is essential that you understand that a child learns something when he is interested and capable; doing it before that happens is only a lesson in frustration and coercion.

What if my child has to take a test?

If your state mandates that your child take a test on certain years, be sure to prepare her. Do many trial runs first so that she understands the process, what is required, what, if any, her time limits are, and all the other details. You may have a child who knows the material inside and out until she goes to write it down on a test, at which point, she freezes. By practicing with her, you can show her how to relax as best she can. If you have a child who reads or writes slowly, you can focus on ways to speed up, since some tests are timed. Many homeschooled children are unaccustomed to testing procedures, institutional settings, and unfamiliar teachers. Help run through the different scenarios with your child (what if she has a question, what if her pencil breaks, what if she has to go to the bathroom?, etc.), and if possible, use a test administrator that is either a homeschooler or an advocate of Homeschooling, so she has a better grasp on how your child might be feeling.

As far as the results of the tests go—sometimes they are never even gathered or requested; some are recorded, and then never commented on; some result (if the child's score is low enough) in a letter. Rarely does a test score cause trouble for homeschooling families, and by now, you are most likely aware that they certainly are not an accurate measurement of what your child does and does not know.

What if my child—or I—hate homeschooling?

Three words: find out *why*. There is a reason and you have to search it out. Do you hate the material? Change it. Do you hate the schedule? Change it. The perk here is that you and your child are the ones in control; if something isn't working, then change it until it does work. The more structured your teaching, the more risk of unhappiness and dissatisfaction on both your parts; consider relaxing your methods. Listen to each other; validate what each one of you is feeling; search for a new solution together.

Is she lonely? Focus on more group activities. Are you swamped with all of the responsibilities of life? Give up those you can, delegate those you will and reorganize those you still have to do. Is he bored? Find out what is interesting to him and focus on that topic for a while. There are solutions out there, and the last one on the list should be giving up and going to public school. Find the reason and find an answer. Ask other homeschoolers; call your state support group; read a homeschooling magazine; attend a conference. Find the solution. It is not giving up.

What if my child is ADD/ADHD?

This topic could fill up a book all by itself—and has. However, this is going to be the abridged version. If this is a specific concern in your family, check out the resources sections for more help.

Picture something for a moment. You are rested, energetic, and surrounded by people you would like to be interacting with. It's a beautiful day and in an hour, you get to go outside and feel the sunshine and *move*. But right now, you have to sit at a desk. Be quiet, Don't talk to anyone around you. Sit still. No fidgeting. No tapping your pencil. No humming. Have to go to the bathroom? Too bad. It's not time and you don't have permission. Oops—the teacher is talking. She is telling you and everyone else about something you recognize as some kind of math. You listen for a moment, but then a gorgeous bluebird flies by the window and you follow it with your eyes as it disappears into the trees. Back to the teacher. Now, you're lost. You missed something and you really didn't' care in the first place. It's hard to follow her when she talks about new stuff. You would much rather read about it or do a worksheet. Actually, right now you really want to tell someone about the great book you read last night or get up and show the class your latest cartwheel. You start to daydream about becoming cartwheel champion in the 2008 Olympics. Your legs start bouncing and your fingers are twitching. You can feel the energy running through your muscles. Sorry to tell you this, but you might have a problem: You might have ADD.

ADD (attention deficit disorder) and ADHD (attention deficit hyperactivity disorder) are very popular labels to put on an increasing number of kids today. Definitions of what it truly is vary from one end of the spectrum to the other. Scientists have defined it as a mental disorder due to a lack of certain chemicals called neurotransmitters in the brain. On the other hand, experts in the world of alternative education have labeled it as "a teaching disability," "a condition created by schools to shirk accountability" and "superior intelligence coupled with inferior self-esteem." So, what is it? Is it a genuine medical problem requiring medication, or just a different way of learning and relating to the world?

The symptoms of ADD are listed below. A child is often diagnosed as having this condition if they have six or more symptoms that last six or more months. Look down the list. Remind you of anyone you know?

- Fidgets
- Restless
- Inability to stay seated
- Short attention span
- Can't wait for a turn
- Loud, noisy, disruptive
- Accident prone
- Daydreams
- Impulsive
- Loses things
- Forgetful
- Driven
- Talks a lot, interrupts often
- Low self-esteem
- Fails to finish things
- Can't concentrate

A great many of these so-called symptoms look to many parents like normal childlike behaviors. Is it too much of a surprise that boys are diagnosed with this condition three times more than girls? If you have a son, you might be shaking your head right now. If you had to write a description of his daily behavior, how many of these symptoms would you list? Does this mean he is disabled, has a deficit, or has a disorder? Or does this just mean that your child is normal? How many of these symptoms are actually signs of being just plain bored?

Consider, for a moment, other possible causes for this type of behavior. Putting aside the concept of a lack of neurotransmitters, how about:

- This is normal child behavior (read that one several times—think it over).
- Diet—too much sugar, caffeine, and artificial preservatives? They can all affect behavior.
- Learning styles—each child learns in his own way. What happens if that isn't how the school/teacher is teaching?
- Allergies—sensitivities to environmental factors
- A phase—his behavior might just be a phase he is going through that will pass

The fact that some children behave differently in school or learning settings is not being disputed; the question is how did this get turned into "disability?" Are we seeing a brand new epidemic among this generation's children or is it something else? Could the schools themselves be playing a role in this diagnosis as they are faced with more children who refuse to—or are unable to—sit still, listen, and learn like the 'normal' child?

Whether or not this type of behavior should be called a disability, it is often treated as such, and many of the children who display such behavior are now being medicated. If you have a child on Ritalin® or if you are thinking that it might be a solution, consider this:

- The drug enforcement agencies "drugs of concern" list Ritalin right there next to cocaine, LSD, and ecstasy.
- Ritalin, or methylphenidate, is a stimulant that is stronger than caffeine.
- The number of preschool children being treated with medication for ADHD tripled between 1990 and 1995.
- The majority of children who receive stimulants for ADHD do not fully meet the criteria for ADHD.

Do you want to try to figure out how to tell your kids not to use drugs, but be sure to take their Ritalin before they go to school? Ritalin may not be the answer for your child's behavior and the consequences of its use can be severe. As parents, it is your right and responsibility to decide whether the doctors and schools are correct and your child does indeed have a condition that requires medication. That's a heavy burden; prepare yourself with as much knowledge as you can. Read, research, and look at both sides of the controversy. Keep in mind two important things: First, in almost every case the schools are operating out of concern for the best interests of your child as they see them; and second, the schools can be wrong. It's essential that you figure prominently in the decision. There's something else to take note of: for many children diagnosed with ADD, schools set up or create an Individualized Education Program (IEP). School systems commonly receive *twice* the state and federal funds for each child with an IEP than they do with a child who is merely "normal."

Homeschooling a child that has been labeled ADD can be one of the best steps you will ever take as a parent. The vast majority of parents who have made this decision report the same thing: within weeks of coming home, nearly every symptom of ADD disappears. They are gone; the parents have found the solution without turning to drugs. The problem was not the child. The problem was the child being put into an environment that was damaging, difficult, and draining.

Parents who homeschool their ADD children have reported that these are the best techniques to use:
- Giving simple, repeated instructions
- Teaching material in the *child's* learning style
- Giving immediate feedback
- Working one on one
- Providing regular and frequent breaks
- Incorporating motion into most activities
- Using a child-centered curriculum based on interests
- Learning everything you can about your child's learning style so you can understand it better
- Keeping the house clear of clutter and excessive noise
- Creating a schedule that a child can understand and follow

Thomas Armstrong, in his book, *The Myth of the A.D.D. Child,* offers many different ways to cope with a child with this label. His list includes:
- Find out what interests your child
- Limit television and video games
- Provide opportunities for physical movement
- Provide hands-on activities
- Use touch to soothe and calm
- Give your child choices
- Provide a balanced breakfast
- Discover your child's multiple intelligences

Often, the child who is labeled with some kind of learning disability in public school is not the victim of a disorder, he simply wants to do something else or at least, wants to do it another way. That isn't wrong; it's an alternative. Here is a list of some people who have been diagnosed or who have been shown throughout history to have exhibited many of the classic ADD symptoms. What do you think of when you read their names? Are these people disabled or just talented? What would the world have missed out on if these people had been drugged instead of allowed to explore and use their abilities?

- Albert Einstein
- Galileo
- Leonardo da Vinci
- Walt Disney
- John F. Kennedy
- Woodrow Wilson
- Louis Pasteur
- Prince Charles
- Beethoven

- John Lennon
- Stephen Hawkings
- Jules Verne
- Alexander Graham Bell
- Hans Christian Anderson
- Thomas Edison
- "Magic" Johnson
- Mozart
- Winston Churchill
- General George Patton

Listen to the perspectives of others: Dr. Martha Denckla, Director of Developmental Cognitive Neurology at John Hopkins, said this about ADD, "Think of an absent minded professor who can find a cure for cancer but not his glasses in the mess on his desk. These are the inventors, creators, poets—the people who think creative thoughts because they don't think like everyone else." Thomas Armstrong, PhD. Writes, "These children are not disordered. They may have a different style of thinking, attending, and behaving, but it is the broader social and educational influences that create the disorder, not the children. I'm alarmed to think that modern science may be turning creativity into a mental disorder." Psychologist Dr. Kathleen Nadeau says, "ADD people are high energy and incredibly good brainstormers. They will often happily work 12-15 hours by choice. The business community should not fear ADD. Instead, they should see that they have a potential gold mine here."

A child who thinks differently, who processes information in more unusual ways, can struggle in public school. The time, the resources, and the budget are rarely available to meet his needs effectively. On top of this, he will have to deal with the negativity that his unique perspective creates from fellow classmates. The different are not tolerated well in public school; he may be labeled different or weird by his classmates, he may be teased, and his self-esteem may suffer. It becomes a Catch-22 situation as his low self-image contributes to his behavior, and his behavior contributes to how he is treated. By bringing this child home, he will have a chance to be himself, without labels and criticism. Think of what this could mean in how he sees himself; by spending his days in a nurturing, loving environment, he may well blossom in ways you never could have imagined.

Keep in mind that your child just may not be ready for a structured school setting of any kind yet. Cindy Wade, author of *Vermont Homeschoolers Directory,* says, "I'm also convinced that children under the age of 10 shouldn't be forced to attend any kind of institutionalized training such as preschool or public school. . . (they) are not psychologically, biologically, emotionally, or physiologically ready for structured learning." If they aren't ready, how can they behave the way the school wants them to? It's like trying to potty train a one year old. He isn't trying to be difficult or obstinate; he isn't able to do what you are demanding of him.

The controversy over ADD continues to rage and you need to do your own research and reading on the topic to figure out how you feel. The key is to become familiar with a variety of perspectives and most of all, to observe your own child closely to see if there is a problem or not. For many children, the best therapy for their so-called disorder is just bringing them back home.

What if my child is special needs?

There are, of course, children who have definite learning issues like autism, Down syndrome, and other physical conditions. The process here is different, and your best resources for information are local and national support groups. They will help direct you to local organizations, conferences, workshops, publications and other important information. However, here is some general information to get you started.

Laws regarding teaching special needs children are different in most states. You will need to find out what they are and how to work with them if they are not particularly lenient. If your children are under the Individual with Disabilities Education Act (IDEA), or you want access to your local schools special services, you must have an IEP.

The first step in this process is evaluation. A panel of experts, with your permission, will examine your child. Usually this group consists of a psychologist, a speech pathologist, a social worker and various medical personnel, depending on your child's needs. They should discuss their assessment with you. It's helpful to brush up on the terminology they are going to use before you meet with them, be sure you know your rights and be ready to take notes.

If the group deems your child to be disabled, then they will partner with you (hopefully) in creating an IEP. In this, they will list your child's present level of educational performance, annual goals for your child, specific ways to determine if objectives are being met, specific services that are to be provided and by whom, when the education will start, how long it will last and how and when they will evaluate for progress.

As you enter into this process, be sure to talk with other homeschoolers in the area for their advice and suggestions. Ask them to recommend books to read, and what they wish they had known before they started homeschooling. Other places to go for help/support include the Developmental Disabilities Planning Council, your state Department of Mental Health, and Mental Retardation and Health and Human Services. You might also want to check in with your local chapter of the National Academy for Child Development or the Learning Disabilities Association of America.

Marsha Ransom, author of *The Complete Idiot's Guide to Homeschooling* writes, "The most important thing you need to know about providing an education program for your child with special needs is to know your child." For additional information, you might also want to contact Pete and Pam Wright. He is a special education attorney and she is a psychotherapist. They specialize in the rights of homeschoolers to receive public school services. Check out their site at www.wrightslaw.com

What if my child is gifted?

Have you ever noticed the incredible similarity between a child who is diagnosed with ADD and a child who is considered to be gifted? If you put the list of behaviors and traits next to each other, it is amazing how much they overlap. Mariaemma Pelullo, a professional learning styles analyst from Reflective Educational Perspectives, wrote, "All children are gifted! In our culture, we define areas in which we think children should be smart and call them 'gifted' when they show the 'right' kind of intelligence, and 'learning disabled' when they don't."

A child who that is labeled "gifted" has usually shown an exceptional ability in one or more areas, whether in reading, art, math, music, or whatever subject. They might exhibit an extraordinary vocabulary, superior reasoning skills, or excellent recall. These children are often extremely bored in school (hence the fidgeting and daydreaming) and like their special needs counterparts, they are labeled as "brains," "eggheads" and other terms for being "too smart." (Remember, the law of the school world is that "different" equals *weird.*)

Homeschooling a gifted child is wonderful; once again, you can tailor his education to his unique needs. Most children who excel in some areas do not excel in all areas, so you might be introducing your 10-year-old to college reading material and then switching over to learning the multiplication tables. If your child is gifted in an area that you are not, or is already beyond your level, you can attempt to reach her level or perhaps hire a tutor or find a mentor. Distance learning programs over the Internet, community college classes and internships are other possibilities. Teaching kids like these may be a combination of helping them with some other weaker areas and sitting back to marvel as they take off in their strongest areas.

At home, these bright children can accelerate as need be without having to pretend to be slower for the sake of their classmates; they can feel normal instead of strange; they can follow their interests and begin to reach their incredible potential. For more resources and support, check out the site www.brightkidsathome.com

In the Trenches

Some Say ~ Melanie Walenciak

Some might say he is impulsive. I say he is eager to try new things. Some might say he is into everything. I say he is curious and loves to discover. Some might say he lacks common sense. I say he is a dreamer and is thinking of things I couldn't even imagine. Some would label him ADD. I name him Cody, and he is my son.

From the start I knew he was different. As a child, he was extremely sensitive to stimuli. He startled at even the slightest of sounds. Trips to the mall were out of the question. His little nervous system simply couldn't handle it.

As he got older, he seemed to require more attention and less sleep. He constantly "read" books about heavy machinery and, at the age of two, would hold captivating, articulated conversations on dump trucks and tunnel boring machines. I received several compliments on my clever little boy.

Somewhere along the line, Cody's strengths began to look more like weaknesses, especially to those that didn't know him. I heard fewer compliments, and more "helpful" suggestions from those who understood my child even less than I did.

"Does he ever stop talking?"
"Have you tried time outs?"
"A good spanking will cure him."
"Maybe he eats too much sugar."

During one particularly stressful week, my husband and I were asked on three separate occasions if Cody had been tested for Attention Deficit Disorder. The idea was shocking, and I refused to accept it. I didn't want to have him tested. I didn't want to limit him with a label. I wanted to focus on what was right, not search for what was wrong.

I made the decision to homeschool well before Cody was born. As his personality emerged, I knew there was no other choice. I could not in good conscience send him to school. He could not sit still for 15 minutes, let alone an hour. On the rare occasion he was able to still his body, his mouth would kick in gear. He would click his tongue and pop his lips. I knew a traditional school would kill his spirit and take away his confidence. I knew he would be told day after day, hour after hour, that something was wrong with him.

So our homeschool journey began.

For a while, things went smoothly. I chose a well-known, expensive curriculum for math and phonics, and used a hands-on unit study approach for all the rest. Cody loved his math manipulatives and played with them everyday. He enjoyed discovering all he could do with them. Phonics was a different story. He knew his letters, but when it came time to code and blend them, frustration levels went through the roof.

I distinctly remember one day we were both close to pulling our hair out. His constant motion wore my patience thin. I knew there was nothing to be done about it at the time. I could expect him to be still or expect him to learn. To do both was entirely out of the question and quite impossible.

On this day, with nerves already frazzled, I asked him a simple review question; he hemmed and hawed and tapped his pencil on the table. He was a very capable staller, but there was no reason to stall this time. I knew he knew the answer, but he would not say it. I became angry and sent him to his room. School was dismissed.

That very evening I had a revelation that changed everything. My husband had cut his finger sharpening a knife. When he asked me where the bandagers were, I could not tell him. I could see the box, sitting in the first aid kit under the sink in the bathroom. I knew exactly where they were, but when I tried to tell him, the words would not come out in any kind of sensible order. In frustration, I finally went to the bathroom and got them myself. The realization hit me hard. This is how Cody feels every day. He knows the answer, but he can't figure out how to get the answer out of his head. And worst of all, it seems he's inherited this dysfunction from me.

Cody took a break from school for a while, and I went back to school, so to speak. I studied learning styles and learning modalities. I studied how the brain works and how our dominant hemisphere affects the way we think and the way we learn.

Most students are left-brained convergent thinkers. That is to say, they are logical and analytical. They appreciate detail and can focus easily on one idea at a time. They thrive on repetition and structure.

It did not take much investigation to discover that Cody was right brain dominant and his thinking was divergent. He prefers the whole picture to the details and lines in a constant state of brainstorm. One idea sparks another, then another, then another. But when he does focus on one thing, he uses hyperfocus. Whether it is heavy machinery at the age of two, or Legos at eight, when Cody is passionate about something, nothing else matters.

I used my newfound knowledge to make several curriculum changes in our home. I sold my phonics curriculum and opted for a whole language approach instead. The coding details of phonics made him hate books, but when I introduced whole words to him, he was able to break down the words and discover patterns for himself. He is now in third grade and reads at a sixth grade level. In fact, he has turned into a voracious reader.

We used his strength in divergent thinking to build his math program. Instead of asking him what 6+6 equals, I asked him to list all the different ways he can come up with the answer 12. In less time than he could focus on 6+6, he brainstorms and comes up with 8+4, 5+7, 10+2, 11+1, 3x4, and 6+6. It is amazing to watch him work.

When learning a new concept, I always present it to him according to his strengths. After he has mastered it, we continue to work with it in a more traditional way, to help him build up his convergent thinking, or focusing skills. He is excelling in ways I never thought possible.

I recently did an Internet search for "divergent thinking" to see what kind of information is available to frustrated parents. What I found surprised me. People are making money teaching others how to think divergently. What is considered a handicap in schools, is now thought of as a commodity in the business world. My heart breaks when I think of all the children in our schools who have this gift, but are told it is wrong and taught to suppress it.

Thomas Alva Edison is a wonderful example of a divergent thinker. As a child he was kicked out of school for being inattentive and a dreamer. His mother knew better and taught him at home. Edison's brilliant mind was nurtured and he became a prolific inventor. He once credited his mother with his success, saying, "She was the only person who truly understood me."

Cody says the same thing about me.

Homeschooling Your Special Needs Child
~ Deborah Bradshaw

My son, Curtis, has Down Syndrome. School was not working for my child for a variety of reasons. He wanted to learn, but he was not learning what he could have been, nor did the school understand how to best meet his needs. My husband saw my frustration and my rising blood pressure and came to the conclusion that we should homeschool.

Although I had personal experience as a schoolteacher and had taught a little of everything—preschool through college, including special education, I was nervous about this prospect and unsure of my ability to teach my own child. Somehow the thought of being solely responsible for his education had me sweating bullets.

I researched the subject and while I found a great deal of information on homeschooling, specific information on homeschooling a special needs child was much more difficult to obtain. I wanted specifics. I finally developed a personal plan based upon my experience as a teacher, but more importantly—on what my child has taught me about the way he learns. These techniques apply to any child, but especially to the child with special needs including Down Syndrome.

When considering any project it is wise to develop a plan. So it is with educating your special needs child. You need a series of steps to determine what your plan will be. Below is a list of suggestions that will help you get started. You will, after working on your plan, find other steps to help you fine tune.

The first step is to determine how your child learns. There are many great books available on learning styles. Some authors list seven styles of learning; others three: visual, auditory, and kinesthetic. I believe there are three basic styles and the remainders are a compilation of these styles and include other factors about the child. Without knowing what style of learning a child has, it is difficult to know how best to present the material.

Visual means the child learns better by a demonstration, or seeing what you are talking about. People who are visual often have trouble remembering people's names but usually remember a face. Visual learners have vivid imaginations, use colors, and often think in pictures. A visual learner will often tell you how they are feeling by their facial expressions.

Auditory learners focus on hearing. They learn well from verbal instruction but are easily distracted by outside noises, people talking, and background noise. Auditory learners benefit from listening and then by retelling.

Kinesthetic learners need to be part of the action. They learn by experiencing, participating in, and doing. Kinesthetic learners are often physically active and impulsive. Manipulatives (items such as counters, labeled photographs, sandpaper letters) and games work well for this style of learner.

The next step in the process is determining what to teach. If the child has been in a public school they will have an IEP or IFSP, Individualized Education Plan or Individual Family Support Plan, respectively. It depends on the child's age as to what plan is typically used. Some states may use different acronyms, but the concept is the same—what does this individual child need to learn to help him best succeed. If your child has been part of the public education system, you are probably familiar with this process.

I was not particularly keen on the idea of an IEP for my homeschooled child. The IEP process was a painful memory for me. It was an experience of telling the school what I wanted for my child and being told it couldn't be done or they did not have the resources, the program, the personnel, and so on. I eventually realized I now had control of the education plan for my child. I could decide what he needed to learn, write my own goals and objectives, and then decide how best to implement the plan—but where would I start?

I needed to determine what my child knew, and more importantly, what he was comfortable enough to use. Sometimes our children know information, they will even repeat it back to us when asked, but being comfortable enough to use it on a daily basis may be a goal yet to be achieved. An example might be, "I know" how to make a chocolate cake. I can list the ingredients and can tell you how hot the oven should be, even how long to bake it. I would, however, not want to make a chocolate cake without the recipe. The same is true for kids with special needs—sometimes they know the "ingredients" it takes to use a particular skill, but they aren't quite sure how it all goes together, they don't quite have the "recipe" memorized.

A child who seems to know how to say words and name objects, but is still unable to carry on a conversation, may have a problem of not having all the building blocks in place to succeed at the task. Sometimes it is okay to use a support until the skill is achieved. In some areas your child may continue to use a support. As adults, we use calculators, encyclopedias, or the Internet to help us with the information we need. It is acceptable for our children to use the tools they need to accomplish the task at hand. Some tools for math might be a calculator, a number line for addition and subtraction, or a printed times table. Use your imagination to come up with creative ideas to help your child further develop their own skills or "recipe."

As adults, our brains are developed to the point we do not often think of the steps involved in learning a new skill. We may even think that we "just learned it." This is because basic skills are learned in a building block pattern. We first learned the basic skills in order to achieve the level we have reached today. An infant does not learn to walk overnight. Human infants typically take nine to thirteen months to learn the incremental skills it takes to achieve the larger goal. First they must learn to control their bodies: roll over, crawl, stand, and so on. The fear of falling may then keep them from moving on to walking when they are physically ready.

Determining a child's current level of skill and confidence can be accomplished in several ways. An assessment test can be given to the child by a licensed physiologist or other qualified professional. An achievement test can be administered depending on the child's level of communication and understanding. It may be simpler, however, to simply observe the child through play and daily life. Keep a record of what the child routinely says, does, and plays. For example, what words does the child use? Is the child able to use scissors or other household objects? Can the child tell you his full name?

This need not be a lengthy project, but one of simple, yet careful, observation throughout the natural day of the child. It is best to observe these skills for at least a few weeks. We all have good and bad days. Some children with special needs are particularly susceptible to days when skills seem to come and go. Do not give up! Simply list those skills as ones to be worked on. I suggest three categories in your observations. Skills already attained (those the child is comfortable in using), skills to be practiced (those which seem to fade in and out), and skills to be attained (skills to yet be achieved). Your observation will provide you with the goals and objectives you need to determine what you will teach. An excellent book that provides lists of incremental and developmental steps is *Behavioral Intervention for Young Children with Autism,* edited by Catherine Maurice, published by PRO-ED, Inc. While this book was specifically written for children with autism in mind, I have found the lists of incremental steps and the suggestions for teaching those steps to be invaluable.

Once you have decided what to teach, you need to find curriculum and materials to accomplish your goals. There are many excellent programs and textbooks on the market. Books, which were previously available primarily to schools, have recently been made more affordable for the homeschooler. Look around; talk to friends about what they use.

Keep in mind that if something doesn't work, it does not mean that the child cannot learn that subject or skill. It may be that the particular method used is not incorporating the student's learning style. It may be the child is not developmentally ready to learn that skill or the building block is not yet in place. Don't give up! It is easy to get discouraged for both you and your child. If something is not working, take a break from it. Be creative. Try something else and come back to it later.

Deuteronomy 11:19 says, "And ye shall teach them your children, speaking of them when thou sittest in thine house, and when thou walkest by the way, when thou liest down, and when thou risest up." This verse makes a good point. If you want your child to truly absorb what you are teaching them, learning must be a continual process. Learning takes place throughout the day, no matter where you may be. It is not confined to the hour we set aside for school.

My son, Curtis, has gained many new skills through our daily life experiences. When we were trying to learn directional words such as up and under, Curtis would help me in the kitchen. I would ask him to get me the pan that is under the stove, bring me the bowl on top of the cabinet, and find the jar that is beside the breadbox. While working on fine motor skills, he cut open packages and helped sort small objects. By having him actually experience these skills, they became part of his working knowledge.

Homeschooling has been a series of ups and downs. Sometimes I think Curtis is not grasping a concept or skill, or that the learning is going too slowly. Some subjects I thought I presented well, but I did not explain as well as I could have. Progress has seemed slow at times, but then when I look back at what he was doing when we began, and when I look at the records from the school, I see just how far we have come. His accomplishments in reading, math skills, and language development have been impressive. More importantly, his self-confidence has increased dramatically. He carries himself differently, he carries on conversations with people he never would have before, and he even walks differently!

You are your child's best teacher and advocate. You have the God-given ability to know your child like no one else can. Do not be discouraged. It is frustrating and difficult at times, but each and every skill gained, and every step accomplished, is worth the effort. As I look back over the past two years and see how much Curtis has gained, I know the decision to homeschool was the best one we could have made.

The Voices of Experience

World Championship Homeschooling ~ Bill Ward

When Cedar Mill, Oregon teenager Rebecca Ward stepped onto the winner's podium at the Senior World Fencing Championships in Torino, Italy in October, 2006, she strode into fencing history. She had already won the Cadet (under 17) and Junior (under 20) World Championships in April. At 16, she now became the youngest fencer ever to win a Senior World Championship, and the only fencer ever to win all three individual titles in a single year. What accompanied her to each of these championship events? A giant backpack bulging with books, a laptop computer and a homeschooling course list.

Rebecca began homeschooling long before her first parry or thrust with a saber. We had had significant experience with the public school system during her older brother William's first three grades. We discovered that typical public school curricula are not well designed for students with exceptional skills in some academic areas, but substandard skills in others. We were aghast at teachers who preferred to let students well above grade level just coast in the areas in which they excelled, languishing until the deficient areas like spelling or handwriting caught up to the mid-stream of the class.

Rebecca entered the 1st grade already math proficient in multiplying and dividing, but challenged in reading, due to some visual integration issues. Testing put her near the top of the charts in math, so when we began home schooling her in the second semester of 1st grade, she qualified for Stanford University's EPGY (Education Program for Gifted Youth) courses in K-6 mathematics. This was an interactive, CD-ROM based course with graphic programs, lectures and tests. She loved the challenge, and was able to blaze through the courses at her own pace. After the first few months, I found myself in the odd position of having to read to her the word problems and instructions on the computer screen. She reveled in the math, but her ability to manipulate numbers far exceeded her grasp of nouns, verbs and phonics.

As she wrapped up the EPGY math program, we began what others called "unschooling." Some of Rebecca's homeschooling acquaintances grimly substituted hours sitting in class with hours sitting at the kitchen table, suffering through what we unschoolers referred to as: "Death by Workbook." In unschooling, the student pursues areas of interest, without regimen or time constraints. If they are working on clay art, and the session goes for 30 minutes or four hours, it makes no difference. If the student is scouring the Internet for information on dolphins, which leads to fish which leads to plankton which leads to 19th century whaling practices, so be it. The process is more about stimulating the natural curiosity to learn, and less concerned with rote memorization of material for a standardized test. The main challenge is always finding creative ways to make sure you get some math, history, science, English and social studies into all the areas of interest being explored. The computer proved to be an invaluable resource, especially during the elementary grades. There are great math, spelling, science, history and reasoning programs available to stimulate young minds.

By the time she was nine years old, Rebecca had developed a love of reading, mainly thanks to our constant parade of bedtime stories and then, Harry Potter. As he did for countless other young readers, the lure of the Potter saga catapulted Rebecca into the joy of reading for herself. It was a bittersweet moment when I finally realized that Dad had been replaced by Hogwarts.

About that same time, Rebecca found a new outlet for the head-to-head competition she had been enjoying in chess: she discovered fencing. Within nine months, she had won her first national competition, and we began traveling to an ever-broader range of fencing competitions around the country. In the early years, fencing meets are divided into age brackets: Y-10, Y-12, Y-14, Cadet, Junior and Senior. As a 10 and under fencer, Rebecca had to place high enough in each higher bracket to be able to continue to fence older and older girls. For instance, national points in Y-12 let her fence Y-14 and on up the ladder. The more events she was eligible for, the more traveling we began to do, and that's where homeschooling really began to play a positive role for Rebecca.

While she was still doing hours of work a day, we could be flexible as to which hours those were. Weekends, evenings after practice, on the plane, in the hotel room… Rebecca set her schedule, not some pursed-lip administrator. Rebecca didn't work off a set curriculum, except for math, where we utilized the Key Curriculum that walked her through the principles of decimals, percentages, geometry and algebra. It was as close to workbook mortality as we would get. For the rest of her studies, we constantly browsed the two homeschooling bookstores in Denver, bringing in texts on as wide a variety of subjects as we could find. Zome Tools were a big hit, as well. Our local homeschooling group also brought in biology labs from time to time. There's nothing like watching a bunch of 11 year olds dissect baby sharks for good clean squeamish fun.

Shortly before Rebecca turned 12, we moved from Denver to Portland, Oregon so she could begin training under the Women's National Saber Team coach, Ed Korfanty. The fencing travel remained constant, with a couple of cross country trips every two to three months, plus the local and regional meets. Then, at 13, Rebecca became eligible for international competition, and a whirlwind of travel began.

Several of Rebecca's teammates had public/private school situations that were not remotely conducive to this much travel: in some cases, after just a excused few absences, the teachers were no longer required to grant leniency for tests or assignments. Even if the fencer was on an excused trip to Ecuador, if they missed the test, the teacher could give them a zero. Our administration was not quite so severe.

Rebecca began carrying all her texts and assignments on the airliner with her, and learned to work in airports and strange hotel rooms. As her math proficiency improved, we stumbled across a most fortuitous asset: math tutor Rupa Houndegla. An Indian immigrant and college instructor, Rupa was recommended highly by a poster on one of the local home schooling boards. We put Rupa and Rebecca together, and it was polynomials at first sight. Within weeks, the two would be giggling together over their math books like two teenagers dissecting *Cosmo* magazine. It was one of the most serendipitous discoveries of her homeschooling career.

As Rebecca began having international success in fencing, and was approaching her high school years, it became apparent that a college fencing scholarship might be possible. While many colleges grant considerable leeway for homeschooling transcripts, the NCAA Clearinghouse—the body which looks at school work and decides whether an athlete is eligible for Division 1 athletic competition—is less flexible. Here, Rebecca's work had to take a more quantifiable turn.

We returned to the EPGY program for English, writing and Physics AP courses, which all generated grades and transcripts. We also found a marvelous program through Duke University: The TIP studies (Talent Identification Program). These online courses mirror high school AP programs in math, biology, anatomy and physiology, psychology, government, academic writing and more. Best of all, these courses have a huge on-line component, as completed course material is handed in over the Internet…so whether Rebecca was in Omaha, Nebraska or Orleans, France, she could keep current on her class work.

As part of her requirements as a homeschooler in Oregon, Rebecca had to register with the state, and take a battery of standardized tests every two years. This is one cautionary area I'd flag for homeschoolers. Public school students are faced with a regular barrage of standardized testing that leads to familiarity and proficiency in taking tests. In many cases, it seems like the ability to learn how to discern what the standardized test is asking in a question is as important as subject matter knowledge. Even though the "teaching to the test" mentality is one of the things many homeschoolers are trying to avoid in their education, they still need to have as much exposure as possible to these kinds of exams, so that the SAT/ACT experience doesn't have such a steep learning curve.

After a handful of tries, Rebecca reached the 90th percentile mark in college aptitude testing, and in 2007 was granted early acceptance into Duke University on a full fencing scholarship. But the schoolwork didn't end there. Rebecca and her three teammates are, as of this writing, in the home stretch of qualifying to compete for the USA in the 2008 Olympic games in China. While her other teammates took a year or more off from their college studies to prepare, Rebecca continues to take a full load of psychology, government, academic writing, Calculus 2 and Spanish courses, with more to come next semester, in order to assure Clearinghouse approval.

It's been a tough few years as Rebecca has struggled to balance international competitions, training, schoolwork and a challenged social life, and it underscores the reality that successful homeschooling has to be, for the most part, self-driven by the student. It is difficult to imagine that Rebecca would have had the opportunities and rewards of international fencing without the ability to homeschool. She's experienced the landscapes, people, culture and foods of 19 foreign countries, all before her 18th birthday.

As they say, not all education takes place in a classroom.

Chapter 8

What are the Legalities?

"How we learn is what we learn."
~ Bonnie Friedman, essay writer

Charting the national homeschooling laws is more than a small challenge because each state is vastly different from another, especially in some of the details of the rules. To demonstrate how diverse the requirements can be, consider this. If a state requires:

• *Testing:* it may be every year, every other year or only once. Some states allow parents to administer the tests; others allow another family member or friend. Still others insist on a certified teacher (many homeschoolers are also certified teachers, so check that possibility out as well). Many times these tests are not necessary if you fulfill other odd requirements as in if one parent is a certified teacher or you are part of a registered homeschool group. There are also states that accept alternatives to standardized tests like portfolios, journals, etc. In other words, if you find out that your state is one that requires testing, don't be discouraged. Get the details.

• *Equivalency:* it simply means that that law requires you to homeschool for a minimum number of days per year, usually between 132 and 188. Sometimes the law will even dictate how many hours a day you have to spend in "school." Don't worry about this; every minute of your child's day can be translated into something educational and meeting this minimum is never a problem for creative minds.

• *Records:* it may mean attendance records or a portfolio or something in between. Simply because they are required does not mean anyone will ever look at them either. Get a teacher's record book at a supply store or create your own online. Keep track of the days (oh look, he's home—check!) and what you do (makes a great scrapbook) and you are set.

• *Registration:* as a homeschooler with the Department of Education and/or your local school district, find out why. Find out what happens if you don't. Weigh your options. Many, many homeschoolers refuse to register so keep it as an option.

• *Notification of intent to homeschool:* it might just come as a casual letter or a routine form that you need to fill out and sign. Some states ask for it once, others annually. Some require little to no information while others ask a lot of questions. Only provide what you legally have to and no more.

• *Curriculum:* this almost always means they want to ensure that you are covering the primary subjects (language arts, math, science, social studies, health, music, art and physical education). Some states may want to add certain subjects and some may even be selective

about what actual materials you use, although this fortunately is rare.
- *Parental competency level*: means the state wants a parent to have at least the equivalency of a GED or high school diploma. Some states require nothing; others require that a parent's education level be at least several grades higher than those they are teaching.

How do I find out what the laws are in my state?

Ask other homeschoolers. Go on the net and Google it. Contact state support groups. Do not—let me repeat that—***do not*** call your local school system or state department of education and ask them. Stop. Read that statement one more time. Most likely they will not know and will give you incorrect information or no information at all. They may even tell you the laws and/or requirements they want homeschoolers to follow other than what the law actually states.

If you do not like your state's homeschooling laws, work to change them. Write letters to your state representatives, attend conferences, start a homeschooling legalities committee or email group, get politically active. Our children's educational rights are vital to the future, so don't be afraid to fight for them.

In the Trenches

Our Self-Education Adventure ~ Letha McGee

From the moment we began our self-education adventure, I knew I had made the correct choice. My son had excelled in institutional school, but my daughter had begun having difficulties, a byproduct of a teacher who was snide and self-righteous rather than nurturing and truly interested in each child's progress. As is my habit, I used the summer after my daughter's fourth grade year to throw myself into learning everything available about homeschooling. I read about school-at-home, Unit Studies, Classical Homeschooling, carschooling, eclectic homeschooling, and unschooling. I read Dorothy and Raymond Moore, David Guterson, John T. Gatto, Cafi Cohen, Tamra Orr, Teri Brown, Jan Hunt, Jennifer Kaufeld, Mary Griffith, Luann Schackelford, Susannah Sheffer, Gordon Neufeld and Gabor Mate, and Grace Llewellyn. Whew. Interestingly enough, though intrigued by Orr's and Llewellyn's embrace of unschooling, I originally dismissed that theory outright as too uncontrolled for my family.

We then started Schooling-at-Home, a method by which one keeps up with what's happening in the institutional schools and follows along, covering all the traditional public school concepts and even using many of the same materials. I'd draw up lesson plans for the morning and for after lunch the next day. I kept a calendar specifically delineating what each child had worked on and for how long. I researched and personally inspected various textbooks to see which felt the best for my use with each child. And I invested in maps, charts, posters, school supplies and manipulatives to give my children the same "advantages" as the kids who remained in public school.

Our school-at-home experiment lasted about a nanosecond.

We were already planning a cross-country move to Oregon for my husband to take a new job. As a family project, we got out United States maps and charted our route. I purchased lined notebooks, gel pens, sparkle pens and crayons so the children could get creative as they journaled their trip cross-country. As we traveled, we studied the changes in soil from region to region. We stopped at Points of Interest to learn regional history of the areas through which we passed. We took a great many pictures: Welcome to the State of New Mexico sign, the Painted Desert, the Grand Canyon, the Great Salt Lake, the city of Boise, the Columbia River Gorge. As we traveled, my feeling of urgency to record and calculate my children's progress naturally fell to the wayside because we were having so much fun.

Prior to setting out on our cross-country trek, I had purchased musical CDs of my favorite artists from my high school and college years. One memorable CD was of Gordon Lightfoot, and I played it and the others several times as we progressed. My daughter became intrigued by Lightfoot's song, "The Wreck of the Edmund Fitzgerald," so I told her what I knew of the actual wreck. Once we arrived in Oregon and moved into our new house, she hooked up the computer and looked up the *Edmund Fitzgerald*. She then began looking into shipwrecks in general - calling me to the computer to read interesting factual stories as she uncovered them. We discovered that there is a shipwreck on the shore of the Northern Oregon coastline, so we planned a trip out to see the *Peter Iredale* wreck. And thus, we were off on our first true unschooling adventure.

The *Peter Iredale* is a 100 year old wreck with a rather mundane history, other than it having permanently landed on the Oregon shoreline just south of old Ft. Stevens. A trip to the area would not be complete without visiting Ft. Stevens with its rich and unique history as the only military installation on mainland American soil actually attacked during WWII. While on our *Iredale*/Ft. Stevens trip, we noticed the light cadence from Cape Disappointment —a lighthouse on the SW edge of Washington, just across the mouth of the Columbia River. That would become the impetus of a later quest of ours to tour the lighthouses of the Oregon coastline!

So that one spark, or kernel of information my daughter found intriguing in an old Gordon Lightfoot song led to our family's quest to visit lighthouses, learn about their various histories, lenses and light cadences, and the lives of the lighthouse keepers and their families during Oregon's earliest years as a state. That led to the study of tides and tidepools, and the volcanic activity of the Cascades. That led to learning the history of the Barlow Pass and Mt. Hood, and Lewis and Clark's Voyage of Discovery. That led to the fascinating history of Timberline Lodge, built during the Great Depression recovery period by otherwise unemployed craftsmen and artists. How does one quantify or test for knowledge gleaned from on-site, hands-on discoveries such as these? So with fresh eyes I reread Orr, Gatto, and Llewellyn's books and decided to take the leap of faith that unschooling demands.

My husband was at first skeptical of this decision. He'd always relied on my self-educated expertise in homeschooling the children and hadn't done a great deal of independent study on his own. I found that I began qualifying to him our outings as "History Lessons" and "Math Lessons." A letterboxing adventure became "Geology Class." Taking the train into Seattle became a study of Puget Sound's wildlife and a study of the Fishing Industry. A trip to the Aquarium became "Life Science." I thought it was my inside secret. But in all truthfulness, there is no better way to learn something than to make it interesting and to get down in the trenches and experience it firsthand! So my fudging of our adventures as "Lessons" wasn't needed. These adventures were actually Life Lessons, with no fudging necessary.

Once my husband's job ran its course and he felt the call to return to our home state to be near family, I joined an online Unschooling support group in the Dallas, Texas, area. Through that group we "met" a family of unschoolers who expressed an interest in the Flat Stanley project my kids were happily pursuing. This Dallas-area family asked us if we'd host their children's Flat Stanleys in Portland, before we sold our home and moved back to Texas. So that last Christmastime, before the house sale closed, we took this family's Flat Stanleys all over Portland: To Pioneer Courthouse Square, to Mt. Hood, to the historic department store Meyer and Frank, on a train ride, crossing the Willamette River and to the Oregon Museum of Science and Industry. Of course, these weren't static photo-ops because we naturally had to explore and experience each venue as a family! We returned the Flat Stanleys to our new online friends, and left soon thereafter for our return trip home to Dallas.

Upon arriving in Dallas, we met our Flat Stanley family in person, and have become wonderful friends. We also have met the other unschooling families from the support group and have moved to a new plane in our self-educating adventures.

We've learned that by trusting ourselves and our children, their own natural curiosity is the best incentive to learn. We've stopped worrying about what is being studied by our children's age peers in institutional school. We've quit making excuses for not having our children in public school, which we've come to view as a children's jail which stifles their inherent curiosity and love of learning, quashes their individuality and decimates their creativity. The positive changes in our family which we've witnessed first-hand since having removed our children from that system are numerous and incredibly varied.

The children don't sabotage each other any longer. They no longer see Mom and Dad as the enemy. They find creative ways to cooperate with each other to achieve their individual goals. They interact with adults and smaller children with no hesitation. Their work ethic is stronger when addressing a desired goal. They make friends because they are interested in others' lives and minds, rather than because those new "friends" can be used toward a selfish goal. They treat everyone, known and unknown, far more respectfully because the people with whom they share their daily activities are either mature individuals or children who have been raised in a similar thoughtful and respectful manner.

As I physically type out this family story here, my teenage daughter is working behind me on the homework she has for a self-selected class to prepare for her admission into community college next

Fall, at the age of 15. She and her brother both take this writing class, as well as a math class to prepare for the college's math entrance exam. They selected these classes, taught by accredited teachers who actually homeschool their own children, so that they could enter college to get the credentials they require to begin their adult lives. They are not locked into the public school curriculum designed to introduce students to set subjects determined by the State School Board, comprised of elected know-it-alls who have their own agendas and biases. Rather, my teens want to follow their own paths and recognize college as their personal path to happiness and security in their adult lives.

My teen son is currently interested in entering the Coast Guard. Though not religious, and certainly not Conservative, he feels he needs to do his part to defend his country and test his physical and mental capacities. He hopes to enter law enforcement once he serves his stint in the Coast Guard. In whatever our children undertake, their father and I trust their judgment, trust them to do their best, trust in their ability to decide for themselves what is important in their own lives, and trust them to find a personal path to their own happiness. We just try our best to open those doors so that the children's paths aren't impeded. We parents aren't teachers. We are facilitators.

Meanwhile, the personal satisfaction I feel about our choice to unschool our family is overwhelming. It's truly a joy to watch your children make wise choices, set personal goals, examine and update their life plans, be good citizens and be excellent and trustworthy companions to friends and to each other.

We no longer shy away from explaining our choice to unschool our family. Having planned, studied, plotted and lived through diverse educational approaches, we know beyond any doubt that our choice has been sound, our approach has made our family relationships stronger, and our children's future security and happiness looks extremely promising. What more can parents hope for?

In the Trenches

Long Pregnancy, Big Baby ~ Nicholina O'Donnell

It is not uncommon for homeschool families to go through a pregnancy while homeschooling. However, it is somewhat more unusual for the pregnancy to last for two years and for the resultant "baby" to be a 52 pound 5-year-old boy. This, though, was our experience.

My husband, Anthony, and I decided to adopt an older child through the foster care system. We made this decision shortly after our daughter, Davan, had her seventh birthday. We had discussed the idea off and on since before she was born, but it was then that we decided we were really going to do it. The whole process started with a phone call and is still on-going in the sense that we, as an adoptive, homeschooling family, are still very much a work in progress.

As I do with whatever my latest obsession is, I threw myself into the process. I finished paperwork in lightning speed. Anthony and I went to classes and completed them as fast as we could. I jumped through every hoop that was presented as quickly and efficiently as possible, dragging Anthony behind me when necessary.

Our homeschool community supported us wholeheartedly and enthusiastically with childcare for Davan while we attended classes, filling out, with amazingly kind words, reference questionnaires with great efficiency and sympathetic ears as the process dragged on and on, much longer than we'd anticipated. I was touched and strengthened by all of the support.

It became a part of our lives, a part of our routines. I had Anthony dictate his answers to the long, involved 40 plus page homestudy questionnaire while he and Davan worked on puzzles together. Davan and I were regular visitors at the local Department of Human Services (DHS), picking up paper work, looking through photo listings, dropping off completed paperwork and all of the other little details involved in adopting, particularly with an older child.

We ran into difficulties and the process dragged on much longer than we'd thought it would. Our case worker was slow to respond and take care of her side of paperwork. Twice, before our homestudy was even completed, I talked with her supervisor. The first time was before we met because we were waiting and waiting to hear from her after completing our classes. The second was when nine months had gone by after we started the process and our homestudy was still not complete.

Finally, after ten months, our homestudy was ready and we were able to look at the dossiers of waiting children. We were so excited and sure we were close to the end. After all, we found seven children when we first looked through the photo listings that we were interested in. One of them had to be a match!

We were surprised to learn that three of the children had already been placed (without the photo listing being updated) and we were turned down for an additional three children as not a good match. The one little boy who was left out of those initial seven, turned out to be more than we felt we could handle, once we learned more about his issues.

We went on, looking at more waiting children, putting in for kids we considered a match, only to be turned down time and again. We'd thought the wait for the homestudy to be complete was difficult, but it was nothing compared to becoming attached, in whatever small way, to so many children and then not having it work out. It was impossible to see the kids' pictures, read about them and not feel some sort of tug with each one.

We finally made it to committee for a seven year old little girl (Davan was now eight), but were not chosen. In Oregon, DHS tries to find three families that are potential matches for each child. Then committee is held by five DHS social workers who are not affiliated with either the child or the families to decide on the best match for the child.

We were, frankly, surprised to not be chosen. We'd been surprised to not go to committee before that, given how many children we'd inquired about. After all, we're a middle class family, with one child, an extra room in the house, with a stay-at-home mom. What was the problem?

We began to suspect that it was that we were homeschoolers. There is a definite leaning toward public school in DHS. We'd heard it over and over again in our training about how good it was for kids to go to school, how to help them succeed there and how to deal with homework. Here we were, a homeschool family. Were we being denied because of it?

We never did find out for certain. We expanded our possibilities by deciding to be open to sibling groups of two, provided that they were the same sex, so that they could share the room we had available. We went to two more committees over the summer, one of which was for a single child and one for a sibling group of two boys. Both times, our hearts were broken. Finally, 23 months after our first phone call to DHS, we were selected for a child. Judea was five-and-a-half and our new son. The hardest part of the whole thing was yet to come – forging a new family with a troubled little boy.

We began visits with Judea and formed a plan between his foster family, his case worker and ourselves as to how the transition to our home would look. Judea moved in before Christmas.

As Judea's case worker indicated we were required to, we signed Judea up to start kindergarten at our local public school after the winter break. We were not excited about this, as we felt that Judea really needed the time with us to bond, plus it frankly put a crimp in our homeschooling lives. We were now tied to a school schedule. However, we figured it was temporary, so we gritted our teeth and did it.

Judea actually did well in school, but was a handful and then some at home. He had more than a little trouble adjusting to a new home. He missed his foster brothers very much. He tested us in many ways.

A few months after Judea joined our family, we decided to start therapy. His therapist, surprisingly, strongly supported pulling him out of school. I say surprisingly because I'd come to expect defending homeschooling to anyone related to either adoption or the school system in any way to be an uphill battle. Judea's therapist is a specialist in working with adoptive kids, who works in a group that exclusively works with foster and adoptive kids. It was a pleasant surprise to have her so strongly in support of homeschooling.

With Judea's therapist's support, we were able to get permission to pull him out of school and we homeschooled him for the remainder of the school year. As we're unschoolers, this really meant mostly a lot of family, bonding time and time for Judea to adjust to our family. This was a great decision for Judea and his kindergarten year.

We did our usual activities including lots of reading, crafts, game groups, book groups, Girl Scouts (with other brothers for Judea play with) and went on lots of trips to the library, science museum, zoo, plays and any other activity that interested us.

What really surprised us, though, was that Judea, even after experiencing both school (albeit kindergarten) and homeschooling (unschooling even!) still really wanted to go to school.

After a very challenging nine months of living as a new family, the school year was upon us. We made the decision to send Judea to school for first grade. Again, this is the right decision for him and our family. He loves school and shines there like he seems to be unable to do at home. Judea and I get a break from the intensity of our relationship when he is in school. With his past hurts centering on mom figures and the anxious attachment he's developed with us, there is a lot of intensity to be sure!

Davan continues to unschool, Judea goes to school and we make it all work. I'm grateful, though, that we're a homeschool family at heart because it gave us a lot of freedom during both the long wait and then with being able to give Judea what he needed. Since Davan is still homeschooled, it gives her a chance for some one on one time when Judea goes to school. It helps her to be more patient with her little brother when he is around. It works, even though I still really dislike being tied to a school schedule!

Is this what we'd envisioned when we made our decision and called up DHS to start this process? No and I am a bit sad about that. I'd really hoped homeschooling would work for my whole family. However, does anything turn out how we think it will? I know I figured my kid(s) would go to school before I had any, but I was a die hard homeschooler by the time Davan was school age. We change and adapt to make things work and make the best decisions we can for our families. Isn't that what led us all to homeschooling in the first place?

About the Author

Tamra Orr is the author of more than 100 nonfiction books but her homeschooling books are her personal favorites. She is mom to four, ranging from 23 to 11 and life partner to Joseph for 25 plus years. Tamra moved to Oregon in 2001 and counts it as one of the all time best decisions of her life.

In the free time that she does not remember having for the last few years, Tamra loves to read, look at the Pacific Northwest mountains, hang out with her kids, watch her husband work on one of his several Volkswagens, and spend time enjoying Joss Whedon series marathons.

Index

ADD/ADHD ... 31, 178
advantages to homeschooling ... 30
ages, different ... 84
alternative schools ... 64
Andersen, John ... 57
apprenticeships ... 64, 142
Armstrong, Thomas ... 181
Bennet, Harold ... 19
Better Late than Early ... *19*
Bill of Rights ... 19
Bradshaw, Deborah ... 188
Brown, Terri ... 130
burnout ... 90
child development ... 41
Christian schools ... 20
classical home education ... 78
Clonlara School ... 26, 113, 125
Coffman, Leanne ... 58
Cohen, Cafi ... 139
Coleman, Dorianne L. ... 67
Colfax, David and Micki ... 20
college ... 7, 142
college degrees ... 61
college prep ... 136
Columbine ... 24
compulsory school attendance law ... 19
computers ... 63, 85
conferences ... 107
Constitution ... 19
costs of homeschooling ... 26, 42
credentials ... 7
critics of schools ... 67
curriculum ... 43, 71, 199
dads homeschooling ... 53
Declaration of Independence ... 19

delayed academics ... 79
department of education ... 21
Deschooling Society ... 19
deschooling ... 74
Dewey, John ... 65
diplomas ... 138
discipline ... 30
distance learning ... 49, 63
divorce ... 51
Dobson, Linda ... 41
documentation ... 83
drama club ... 144
driver education ... 50, 144
dual enrollment ... 49
equivalency ... 199
extra-curricular programs ... 50
family bonds ... 24
famous homeschoolers ... 27
Farenga, Patrick ... 8, 61
field trips ... 106
financial security ... 65
Fixing Columbine ... 67
flexibility ... 42
Frames of Mind ... 75
friends ... 171
Gardner, Howard ... 75
Gatto, John Taylor ... 41, 73
grade levels ... 84
grades ... 73
graduation ... 139
grandparents ... 119
Greer, Bill ... 97
Griffith, Mary ... 81, 85
Growing without Schooling ... 8, 19
Harvard college ... 143
Hegener, Mark ... 36
Hendrickson, Borg ... 122
Hepburn, Claudia ... 43
Heuer, Loretta ... 83

Hoagland, Carolyn 126
Holt Associates 8, 61
Holt, John 7, 19, 64, 67, 80
Home Education Magazine 19, 21, 27, 139
Home Grown Kids 19
homeschoolers, numbers of 20
How Children Fail 19
Illich, Ivan 19
improving education 61
independent study 49
Instead of Education 19, 64
international homeschooling 27
Internet 63, 85, 86
internship 142
Ishizuka, Kathy 80
isolation 109
journals 83
Kaseman, Larry 21, 139
Kurdi, Patty 92
later learning 79
laws 26, 100
learning disabilities 31
learning styles 30, 75
Lee, Martha 28
Llewellyn, Grace 27
Mann, Horace 65
Mason, Charlotte 79
Massachusetts 19
materials for homeschooling 71
McCarthy, Mary 89
McGee, Letha 100
minority families 27
misconceptions 25
Montgomery, Pat 113, 125
Moore, Dr. Raymond 19, 79
motivation 90
moving 173
myths 25
No More Public School 19
notification 199

O'Donnell, Nicholina 205
objections, dealing with 119, 122, 125
orchestra 144
parental roles 52
part time homeschooling 48
Perchemlides v. Frizzle 20
philosophies 77
portfolio 83
prom 140
public school and homeschooling 48
public school model 21
qualifications to homeschool 41
questions, answering 123
Ransom, Marsha 184
reading 176
reasons to homeschool 22
records 83, 199
registration 199
relatives 56, 119
relaxed approach 90
religion 23, 25
report cards 83
research 21
researcher 61
resources for homeschooling 71
roles of parents 52
safety 23, 65
schedules 83
scholarships 144
School can Wait *19*
school officials 109
school, withdrawal from 46
self-education 100
Sherman, Rita 66
short term homeschooling 72
siblings 24, 85
Silberman, Charles 67
single parents 51, 58
Sizer, Ted 67
social change 67

socialization 26, 29, 44, 57
special needs 183, 188
sports 144
starting homeschooling 82
statistics 20
stay at home dads 52
Stillwell, Francy 111
stress 90
structured homeschooling 78
subjects, teaching 86
successful in school 50
support groups 103
support, lack of 119
Teach Your Own *19*
teacher homeschooling 111
teenagers 135
television 85
testing 29, 81, 88, 177, 199
textbooks 29
Time magazine 20
time, how much to homeschool 41
traditional homeschooling 78
transcripts 83
unit studies 79
Unschooling Handbook 81
unschooling 41, 80
Viator, Susan 31
violence in schools 20, 24
Virginia Tech 24
volunteering 64, 141
Walenciak, Melanie 185
Ward, Bill 192
Wood, Peg 93
working and homeschooling 46
year round homeschooling 82

Resources

Home Education Magazine
http://www.homeedmag.com

Published continuously since 1984, *Home Education Magazine* is the most widely recommended publication available for homeschooling families. Each issue includes several feature articles; interviews with today's most interesting homeschool personalities; and outstanding columnists writing about topics of interest to homeschooling families. Also news reports, letters from readers, reviews, resources and much more! If you only purchase one resource for homeschooling your children, make it *Home Education Magazine*!

HEM's Books on Homeschooling
http://homeedmag.com/catalog/books.html

"Where do we start?" "How can we find the best resources?" "How can we teach everything our kids need to know?" "What about a high school diploma and going on to college?" We offer these carefully selected homeschooling books for continued support of your family's homeschooling!

Call toll-free: 1-800-236-3278, email Info@homeedmag.com (be sure to include your name and address).

Postal mailing address:
Home Education Magazine
Post Office Box 1083
Tonasket, WA 98855-1083

Free Services & Resources For Homeschooling

Home Education Magazine's Free Services
http://www.homeedmag.com

An award-winning website offering many helpful and supportive free services to homeschoolers, including:
* HEM's News & Commentary - Up-to-date News and Analysis!
* HEM Takes a Closer Look - Exploring issues and resources
* HEM's free Introduction to Homeschooling booklet
* Great reading, timely news, and updates at the HEM Weblogs
* The HEM News - Free email newsletter, back issues are archived
* Networking with other homeschoolers via our free discussion lists
* HEM's Back Issues Archives: Articles from 25+ years of HEM

* Our popular themed Back Issue Packages on specific topics
* FAQs, Questions & Answers - An in-depth collection
* HEM's large selection of recommended books on homeschooling
* Information About Subscribing, Back Issues, special packages, etc.

The American Homeschool Association
americanhomeschoolassociation.org

The American Homeschool Association is a network of homeschoolers working to support homeschooling by providing an online point of contact for news and information, resources and encouragement. The AHA web site offers:

* FAQs & Information for New Homeschoolers - What to do if this is a whole new idea for you
* Articles, Essays, Editorials - The best writings on dozens of topics
* The History of Homeschooling Series - Perspectives on where we've been, and where we're going as homeschooling families
* The Kaseman Columns - Homeschooling issues and political action from the pages of HEM
* Interviews with Homeschool Personalities - Book authors, conference speakers, newsmakers and many others
* Resource Links - Thousands of resources, from all the best sources
* Book Reviews, Authors' Sites, and Book Lists - Reviews, recommendations and much more
* Support Groups & Organizations - Support, networking, conferences, resources, and more
* Websites We Like - Click to these favorites for more information about homeschooling
* AHA's Free Email Discussion Lists - News, views, and networking with other homeschoolers
* Favorite Quotes and Excerpts about Homeschooling

Order additional copies of this book from:

HEM Books, Post Office Box 1083, Tonasket, WA 98855-1083
1-800-236-3278; Info@homeedmag.com
http://homeedmag.com/catalog/books.html